ROLLS~ROYCE

STATE MOTOR CARS

ROLLS~ROYCE

— STATE MOTOR CARS —

ANDREW PASTOUNA

**The publishers would like to thank Warren Allport
for his contribution to this volume, including all captions to illustrations,
plus additional information and photographs.**

**With grateful thanks to Rolls-Royce Motor Cars Limited and the Rolls-
Royce Enthusiasts' Club, The Hunt House, Paulerspury,
Northamptonshire, for information and illustrations.**

First published in Great Britain in 1995 by Osprey,
an imprint of Reed Consumer Books Limited,
Michelin House, 81 Fulham Road, London SW3 6RB
and Auckland, Melbourne and Singapore

ISBN 1 85532 440 7

Project editor Shaun Barrington
Editors Warren Allport and Julia North
Page design Leigh Jones

Printed in Italy
by G. Canale & C. S.p.A. - Borgaro T.se - TURIN

CONTENTS

HEADS OF STATE
ROLLS-ROYCE MOTOR CARS

Although it is well over a century since the first practical demonstration of the internal combustion engine as a means of propelling a carriage, it was not considered to be a reliable, or – in some ways more germanely for this book – respectable form of conveyance until well into the 1900s. Even the birthplace of the motor car, Germany, did not enjoy the patronage of the Head of State – Kaiser Wilhelm II – until after his first ride in a Cannstatt-built Daimler in 1903. Curiously his uncle, Edward VII, had ordered his first motor car – a Coventry-built Daimler – in the closing year of the previous century. When Edward VII felt that his Daimler was both reliable and respectable enough to use for undertaking public engagements in 1904, his nephew, the Kaiser, followed suit and started to use the car on public business.

Across the Atlantic, where the petrol engine was enjoying widespread acceptance, it was not until 1909 that The White House ordered petrol-engined vehicles, and indeed it was another dozen years before these Pierce-Arrow cars supplanted the stable entirely. By this time, the motor car had gained widespread acceptance around the world by Heads of State as entirely suitable for their duties.

Although arriving relatively late onto the world markets as a motor car manufacturer, in 1904, Rolls-Royce established a very special niche for itself in a relatively short space of time. Before the decade was out, few Heads of State could resist reinforcing their public authority by riding behind the radiator of the motor car claiming to be The Best In The World.

Generally speaking, any vehicle carrying the Head of State on official business can be said to be a State Car. However, the purpose of this book is to record those vehicles conceived as State transport and built with that purpose in mind. The specialised formal coachwork embraces a variety of styles from the massive limousine to the stately landaulette and the elegant four-door cabriolet.

The purpose of such designs was to enable the occupant to be seen,

Over three decades of Danish royal motoring separate the two Rolls-Royces at the royal garages in Copenhagen. Their warranty documentation differs considerably in appearance but still confers a three-year guarantee.

provide a comfortable environment and allow a certain amount of security. The chassis manufacturers were responsible for mechanical reliability; with the variety of climatic conditions and occasionally indifferent servicing these vehicles had to endure, this was a challenge. Assassinations of Heads of State have occurred, of course, whilst the representative is being driven on public duty. Just after the first decade of this century, the Austrian heir to the throne was assassinated in a Graf & Stift cabriolet at Sarajevo. Twenty years later the King of Yugoslavia was murdered in the back of a Delage landaulette in Marseilles and, of course, everyone can remember the agonising loss of President Kennedy in Dallas, 1963 – this was in a Lincoln Continental. Only one such terrible event has happened in a Rolls Royce – in the early fifties, when the Governor of Malaya was shot. Such a threat has been an additional challenge to the chassis and coachbuilders.

Rolls-Royces have always enjoyed longevity, and many such state cars are still in use and quite a few are entering their fifth decade in the public eye. This is their story.

EUROPE

BELGIUM

I t was unlikely that Rolls-Royce would make any impact on the State motor fleet in Belgium until the renowned car manufacturer Minerva ceased production in 1940. The company had enjoyed patronage from the Belgian Royal Family between the world wars. They found the big sleeve-valve engines perfectly suitable, as did King George V across the Channel. With the return of peace in 1945, however, an opportunity existed to purchase elsewhere. Although Mercedes-Benz was struggling to re-enter the car market, it was evidently a policy in the immediate post-war days for the Belgian Royal Family to look beyond Belgium's border.

The fate of the occupants of the Laeken Palace in Brussels was, however, very much in doubt. For reasons that lie outside the scope of this book, Leopold III was made a scapegoat by the British Government for the surrender of his army to the Nazis in late May 1940. This situation had been brought about by the decision (not communicated to the Belgian King) that, to save the British Expeditionary Force, evacuation would begin from Dunkirk. The plan was not communicated officially for seventy-two hours; Leopold had been abandoned by the British Army and had no other ally. On reflection, the King should perhaps have followed Queen Wilhelmina's example and fled to Britain, but he stayed on and was viewed by many as having surrendered his army without prior consultation, although, in fact, the reverse was true. In subsequent years, George VI of Britain – who knew the whole story – resisted enormous pressure to remove King Leopold's name from the Roll of the Knights of the Garter.

With the return of the allied army to Belgium in 1944, Leopold III retired to private life and a regency was established under his brother Prince Charles. This was only a temporary solution and Belgium had to wait until Prince Baudouin reached twenty in 1950 to become Prince Royal and King a year later. The brothers Leopold and Charles lived out the remainder of their lives in quiet obscurity. During his six years as Belgian Head of State,

Prince Regent Charles decided to patronise the company whose aero engines had played such a crucial role on the recent conflict – Rolls-Royce.

The first choice for Prince Charles was a pre-war Phantom III, chassis 3BT 131. This has been bodied by the old established Belgian coachbuilder Vesters & Neirinck for the Brussels Motor show of 1937. They constructed a six-light limousine with a quite pronounced sloping windscreen (a special feature of the coachbuilder) and twin side-mounted spares. Originally the chassis had been shipped to Brussels in April 1937 where it was sold to a Madame Jacqmotte after an exhibition. The car survived the war and was acquired by the acting Head of State in July 1945. The last known whereabouts of the Phantom III was when it was sold at a Christie's auction held in Holland in November 1975 for the sum of BFL35,000.

HRH The Prince Regent ordered three post-war chassis – one was bodied by H.J. Mulliner, one by Park Ward and the third by the Belgian coachbuilder Van den Plas. The first chassis is believed to be WVA 12 (though in researching for this book, we could not confirm the chassis number in the H.J. Mulliner records) and was a derivative of Design 7062, a touring limousine. For the Prince Regent, however, H.J. Mulliner omitted the centre division and the body emerged purely as a saloon, with no centre cabinet-work. Curiously, it was one of only two built to this saloon specification. It was a four-light elevation and had its guarantee card issued in May 1947.

Chassis number two was WVA 41, and Prince Charles turned to Park Ward for a limousine style. This was their first post-war formal design and was allocated number seventeen. It has to be said that this was not one of Park Ward's most imposing creations; there were to be five limousine designs within a dozen years which were all, frankly, uninspiring. So bad was Design 17 that it was redrawn within twelve months. The limousine was fitted with an electric division, electric backlight blind, radio behind the division, face-forward occasionals and a sideways-mounted footrest. The Park Ward Silver Wraith limousine was shipped to Brussels at the end of December 1947, and the guarantee was issued in January 1948.

The third and final chassis was clothed with a four-door body outside Great Britain by the famed coachbuilder Van den Plas. It was to be one of their last commissions. Originally this Belgian firm had premises in Brussels, and then Antwerp, where they had begun building complete coachwork in

1884. A new Brussels works was built in 1903 and a licensed London branch operated from 1913. Following the First World War it was restructured as VandenPlas (England) Ltd but faced increasing competition and was sold by the Receiver in 1923. The new VandenPlas (England) 1923 Ltd, under different British management, went on to build many fine bodies and survived at Hendon until 1979. The original Belgian coachbuilder also prospered and was responsible for excellent bodies. Following the the Second World War, though, Van den Plas saw that the future of separate body-building was limited and entered their final phase. Almost their last coachbuilt chassis was on Rolls-Royce, at the command of the Prince Regent.

Rolls-Royce were naturally rather late to produce the first of their post-war Silver Wraith chassis; 1946 ended with only two cars delivered. Despite this, a chassis was allocated for the Belgian order and it began its journey to Brussels for bodywork in the middle of August 1947. It was to be virtually a year before the guarantee card was issued on 4 August 1948. Rather unusually for its time, the body was constructed entirely of steel, apart from the engine bonnet which was aluminium. Park Ward had pioneered this method on their successful Bentleys before the war. Van den Plas proceeded with the building, under the guidance of one of the family directors who had come out of retirement for the job. Each small body section was hot hammer welded and the detail extended to the design of the concealed door hinges and the operation of the side windows which were made to operate on rollerbearings set into brass guides.

The completed Silver Wraith, chassis number WYA 5, was painted in a Royal Brown, with complementary leather upholstery. A radio was fitted and, rather unusually on so early a post-war car, double-filament headlamps; a separate switch operated the centre passlamp. The car was registered with the Palace numberplate 4. However, the VandenPlas cabriolet was only destined to remain in the Royal garage for a relatively short time and was disposed of just under two years later, on 4 August 1950 to a relation of Prince Regent Charles. The car remained with the family until 1968, when it was acquired by Baroness Warnant.

In 1973 it was acquired by an eminent North American collector who has half a dozen exotic Rolls-Royce and Bentley vehicles in his possession. Perhaps the most astonishing feature of chassis WYA 5 is that in over

Prince Regent Charles of Belgium took delivery of this Silver Wraith
cabriolet in 1948. The all-steel body was by the Belgian coachbuilder
Van den Plas. The whitewall tyres were unusual at that time.

forty-five years the car has recorded a mere 10,100 miles and is
believed to be still on its original tyres. The word 'unique' is quite often
wrongly applied, but surely this is true of this most unusual coach-built
Silver Wraith.

It is sad to record that, with the departure of the Prince Regent
Charles in the summer of 1950, Rolls-Royce cars slowly disappeared from
the Royal garages. His successor, King Baudouin, was a particularly
modest man who never showed much interest in prestigious and exotic cars.
Today the early post-war Belgian Rolls-Royces remind one of the brief spell
they enjoyed as transport for the Head of State.

DENMARK

It is curious that Rolls-Royce, who had started serious production of the famed Silver Ghost in 1907, had to wait half a century before an order was placed by the Danish Royal Court. However the Danish Monarchy had for quite some time patronized the Bentley marque. After the Second World War, Frederik IX had quite a number of these, all drophead coupés, purchased in 1950, 1956, 1960, 1965 and the final one in 1967.

In the autumn of 1957 there came a change of policy. His Majesty decided to acquire a suitable State car and he turned to the British coach-builder who over the years had provided many of the State vehicles for Heads of State. Hooper & Co were approached to construct rather urgently a body based on design 8460. This was a standard limousine which went through several small modifications and had been introduced on the Silver Wraith long wheelbase chassis in 1952. The only external difference was introduced at the 1956 Earls Court Motor show when built-in headlamps became part of the specification. Until the end of the limousine run in 1959, the bodies were a composite construction of light alloy and English ash with aluminium panels. The chassis also had the 4,887cc engine with twin SU carburation and a raised 8:1 compression ratio.

The order was placed through the Scandinavian Motor Company in the first week of November 1957. The extensive specifications included a roof aerial, a rear radio with an extension speaker in the front, a speedometer in kilometres, high frequency horns, a button in place of the mascot (which was supplied loose), a British-type rear number plate and a spare parts kit supplied by Rolls-Royce's Hythe Road servicing centre. The standard electric drop division was installed, with self-cancelling switches fitted on either side of the rear seat and provision for operation by the driver. By this time all post-October 1956 limousines were available with power-assisted steering at extra cost and this soon became standard equipment on the Silver Wraith chassis.

Chassis LGLW 25 was delivered to Hooper's Western Avenue coach-works just before Christmas and work was accelerated to finish the limou-

Specification for the Hooper limousine ordered in 1957. The standard limousine was based on design 8460, mounted on the Silver Wraith chassis. Built-in headlamps were part of the standard specification from 1956.

HOOPER & CO
(COACHBUILDERS) LTD

RETAILERS OF BENTLEY, DAIMLER & ROLLS ROYCE CARS

54 ST. JAMES'S STREET, PICCADILLY
LONDON, S.W.1

TELEPHONE : HYDE PARK 3747.   TELEGRAMS : SOCIABLE LONDON

Specification

Specification No. 1017

Design No. 8460

HOOPER 7-SEATER LIMOUSINE
ON ROLLS-ROYCE SILVER WRAITH

SEATING	Fixed front seat. The rear seat, fitted with a folding centre armrest, accommodates 3 persons. 2 facing forward occasional seats folding against the rear of division.
CONSTRUCTION	Composite construction of light alloy and English Ash, completely panelled in aluminium; incorporating fume, sound, draught and dust prevention principles.
DOORS	Four, front doors hinged on the front pillars and rear doors on the rear pillars, all fitted with slam locks, concealed hinges and door checks.
PRIVATE LOCKS	Nearside doors fitted with private locks, remainder with catches fastened from interior.
WINDOWS	Division window to drop, electrically operated and controlled from front and rear compartments. Permanent chromium plated metal frames to all other windows. Door windows to drop manually operated, Quick-lift to driver's window. Pivotted ventilating panels to front doors; hinged quarter windows.
WINDSCREEN	In one piece permanently fixed.
SAFETY GLASS	Triplex laminated glass to windscreen and backlight, toughened Triplex glass to windows.
WINGS AND STEPS	Aluminium front wings merging into the body sides and concealing the running boards. Lightweight detachable covers over the rear wheels.
BOOT	Door hinged at lower edge forming a platform for luggage when folded down.
PAINTING	Cellulose to choice of colour.
UPHOLSTERY	The interior trimmed in " West of England " cloth to choice; front compartment trimmed in leather.
CABINET WORK	Polished wood cabinet fitted in centre of rear of division. Interior woodwork and instrument board in polished veneers to choice.
VENTILATION AND HEATING	Variably controlled inlet for supply of fresh air to the front compartment. Heater to front and rear compartments.
INTERIOR LIGHTS	Two electric roof lamps to the rear compartment and two to the front, operating automatically with the opening of the doors; all provided with independent switches.
INTERIOR FITTINGS	Cigar lighters, ashtrays and ascending handles to front and rear compartments. Two sun visors, cubby holes in instrument board; swivel " pull-ups " on each side of rear seat.
STANDARD EQUIPMENT	Two Lucas headlamps built into front wings, side lamps, stop-tail lamps and reflectors, reversing lamp, flashing direction indicators.
	Twin electric horns, radio, demister to windscreen and backlight, dual bladed screen wiper, screen wash equipment, instruments, lock to petrol filler door.
	Front and rear bumpers, spare wheel below boot floor, jack, kit of tools and spares.

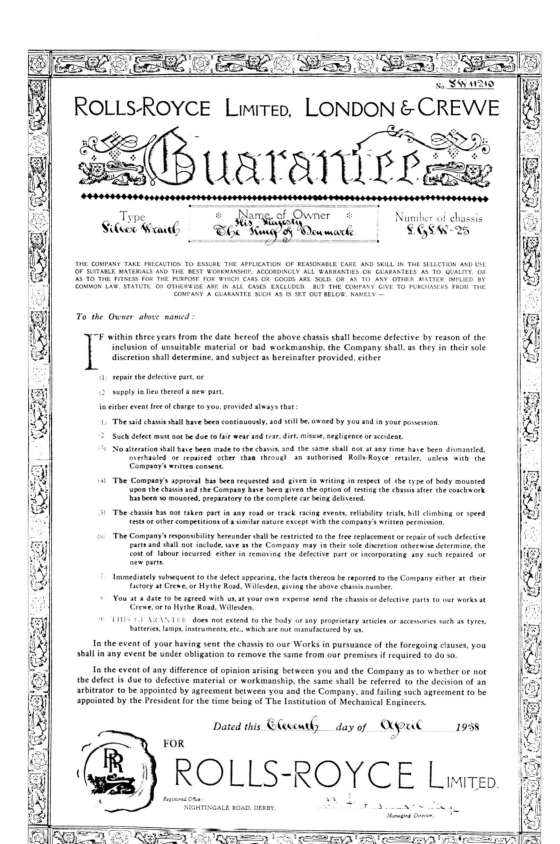

No. 8811210

ROLLS-ROYCE LIMITED, LONDON & CREWE

Guarantee

Type	Name of Owner	Number of chassis
Silver Wraith	*His Majesty* *The King of Denmark.*	*L.G.L.W.-25*

THE COMPANY TAKE PRECAUTION TO ENSURE THE APPLICATION OF REASONABLE CARE AND SKILL IN THE SELECTION AND USE OF SUITABLE MATERIALS AND THE BEST WORKMANSHIP, ACCORDINGLY ALL WARRANTIES OR GUARANTEES AS TO QUALITY, OR AS TO THE FITNESS FOR THE PURPOSE FOR WHICH CARS OR GOODS ARE SOLD, OR AS TO ANY OTHER MATTER IMPLIED BY COMMON LAW, STATUTE, OR OTHERWISE ARE IN ALL CASES EXCLUDED. BUT THE COMPANY GIVE TO PURCHASERS FROM THE COMPANY A GUARANTEE SUCH AS IS SET OUT BELOW, NAMELY:—

To the Owner above named :

IF within three years from the date hereof the above chassis shall become defective by reason of the inclusion of unsuitable material or bad workmanship, the Company shall, as they in their sole discretion shall determine, and subject as hereinafter provided, either

(1) repair the defective part, or

(2) supply in lieu thereof a new part,

in either event free of charge to you, provided always that :

(1) The said chassis shall have been continuously, and still be, owned by you and in your possession.

(2) Such defect must not be due to fair wear and tear, dirt, misuse, negligence or accident.

(3) No alteration shall have been made to the chassis, and the same shall not at any time have been dismantled, overhauled or repaired other than through an authorised Rolls-Royce retailer, unless with the Company's written consent.

(4) The Company's approval has been requested and given in writing in respect of the type of body mounted upon the chassis and the Company have been given the option of testing the chassis after the coachwork has been so mounted, preparatory to the complete car being delivered.

(5) The chassis has not taken part in any road or track racing events, reliability trials, hill climbing or speed tests or other competitions of a similar nature except with the company's written permission.

(6) The Company's responsibility hereunder shall be restricted to the free replacement or repair of such defective parts and shall not include, save as the Company may in their sole discretion otherwise determine, the cost of labour incurred either in removing the defective part or incorporating any such repaired or new parts.

(7) Immediately subsequent to the defect appearing, the facts thereon be reported to the Company either at their factory at Crewe, or Hythe Road, Willesden, giving the above chassis number.

(8) You at a date to be agreed with us, at your own expense send the chassis or defective parts to our works at Crewe, or to Hythe Road, Willesden.

(9) THIS GUARANTEE does not extend to the body or any proprietary articles or accessories such as tyres, batteries, lamps, instruments, etc., which are not manufactured by us.

In the event of your having sent the chassis to our Works in pursuance of the foregoing clauses, you shall in any event be under obligation to remove the same from our premises if required to do so.

In the event of any difference of opinion arising between you and the Company as to whether or not the defect is due to defective material or workmanship, the same shall be referred to the decision of an arbitrator to be appointed by agreement between you and the Company, and failing such agreement to be appointed by the President for the time being of The Institution of Mechanical Engineers.

Dated this *Eleventh* *day of* *April* 1958

FOR

ROLLS-ROYCE LIMITED.

Registered Office:
NIGHTINGALE ROAD, DERBY.

Managing Director.

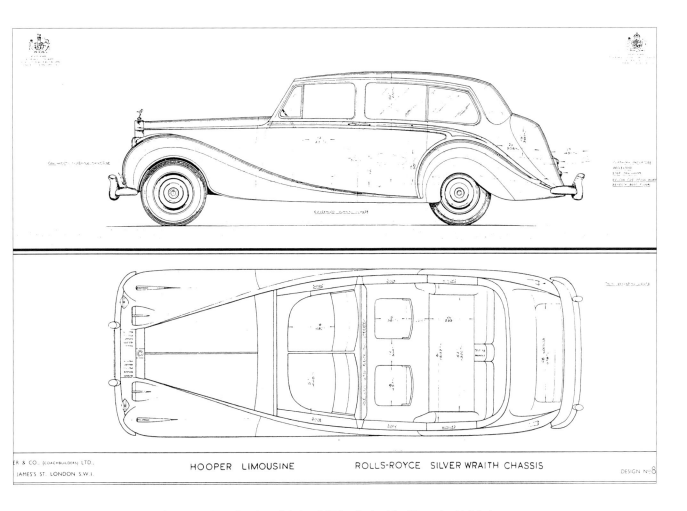

HOOPER LIMOUSINE   ROLLS-ROYCE SILVER WRAITH CHASSIS

ER & CO., (COACHBUILDERS) LTD.,
JAMES'S ST. LONDON S.W.1.

DESIGN N° 8

ABOVE: *Line drawing of design 8460 submitted by Hooper's chief designer,*
Osmond Rivers, to His Majesty King Frederik IX of Denmark.
LEFT: *The Rolls-Royce guarantee certificate for King Frederik's Silver Wraith*
covered only the chassis.

sine on time. The left-hand-drive chassis was ready to receive its bodywork early in the new year, when work began on glazing, cabinet-work and upholstery. The Silver Wraith was painted black with twin white picking-out lines. The normal rear cabinet was deleted, enabling the seats to meet in the centre. As was usual in this type of car, leather was used for the front compartment and cloth in the rear. By early February, Rolls-Royce was told that the limousine was ready for testing and later that month the vehicle was shipped to Copenhagen. On arrival, two painted crowns were fitted on shields and can be viewed on the front and rear aspects of the limousine.

ABOVE: *A crown on a shield is affixed in place of number plates on
the Danish Royal limousine, which is garaged at the Christiansborg
Palace. Thermostatic radiator shutters give this unusual appearance
when the engine is cold.*

RIGHT, TOP: *In Queen Margrethe II's ownership repeater flashers
were added to the front wings. The flag masts were an earlier addition
in 1963.*

RIGHT, BOTTOM: *Hooper's limousine design with large rear side
windows and small rear quarter panel ensures the occupants
are visible on State occasions. Obviously, this is a prime consideration
for any automotive design conceived primarily for public visibility
of the occupants.*

ABOVE: *After over three decades of Danish Royal service the Silver Wraith has now been joined by a new Silver Spur.*
RIGHT: *The Danish Royal crest (right) appears on the rear doors.*

The guarantee card was issued in the name of The King of Denmark and took effect from 11 April 1958. In 1963, flagmasts were added to the car and in recent years the car has been serviced at the official Rolls-Royce workshop at Bert Hansen Glerupvej in Copenhagen.

For over 35 years the limousine has undertaken all the main engagements of the Danish Royal Family. The one change of ownership was in January 1972, when Queen Margrethe II succeeded to the Danish throne. The only obvious modification was the installation of repeater flasher units on the front wings, in front of the rear view mirrors. Chassis LGLW 25 has now completed 120,000 kms (75,000m). The Silver Wraith is kept at the

The 1994 Silver Spur III is a long wheelbase saloon, carries the Danish number 101 and is more suited to less formal use than the the Silver Wraith; a modern car for a modern parliamentary monarchy – but still a Rolls-Royce.

Christiansborg Palace and is still considered to be the principal car for the Queen and Prince Henrik on official and State visits. In addition, in early 1994 a Silver Spur III longwheelbase saloon was acquired for the Danish Royal Household.

GREECE

The Greek Royal Family always led a rather precarious existence. The dynasty was only founded in 1863 and had its origins in the Danish Royal Family. When the House of Glucksborg provided a bride, Queen Alexandra, for Britain's Edward VII the House became united by marriage with the Greek Royal Family. From the beginning of this century they were to face much misfortune; monarchy to republic, republic to monarchy, a change of king and finally a close decision in the 1970s to become a republic.

The Greek Royal House is believed to have acquired its first Rolls-Royce in 1929. King George II (not a direct descendant, but elected by a Revolutionary Committee in 1923), acquired a car that had originally been built on a 20hp Rolls-Royce (chassis 48 GO) by the Manchester coachbuilder Cockshoot. This was a small landaulette, to their design 961, which had been submitted to their client in February 1923, and handed over to the owner the following June. The subsequent fate of the vehicle is not recorded. However, the fate of the Greek Royal Family has been, and it was was really quite dramatic. After Greece's entry into the Second World War, the family fled to Egypt in 1941, and after the war's end a communist putsch raged, following which the monarchy was restored in 1946.

Whilst in exile in Cairo, the Greek Royal Family became closely associated with a wealthy businessman, Theodore Cozzika, who had acquired two Rolls-Royces which he offered to the exiled King as suitable transport. Both the Phantom IIIs (chassis 3DL 102 and 3DL 142) were saloons with a division. Chassis 3DL 142 was originally destined for a Czech coach builder, but the war meant that this was not to be, and the body was finished by H.J. Mulliner. The design number was 6304 which, in the jargon of the day, was called 'a high vision model'. Both Phantoms had Perspex panels in the front portion of the driving compartment. A glass section was installed in the roof of 3DL 142, some way behind, which could be covered using a manual shutter.

Both cars were shipped from Egypt to Greece just after the restoration and were used principally as State cars. His Majesty was keen to own an open car, but Greece's finances in the immediate post-war years were of course disastrous. In late 1949, the new King Paul decided that it would be

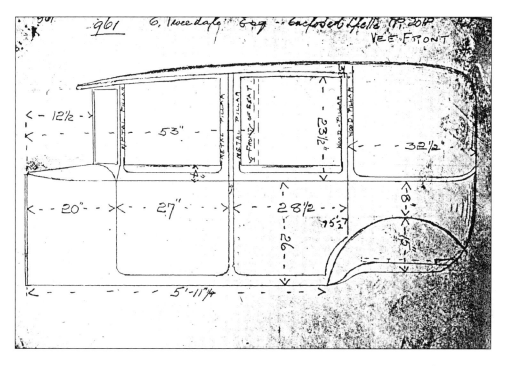

TOP: *The annotated drawing prepared in February 1923 by Cockshoot to show the various dimensions of the enclosed landaulette body ordered by Ernest Tweedale for a Rolls-Royce 20hp chassis.*
ABOVE: *The completed Rolls-Royce 20hp, chassis 48 GO, delivered to its first owner in June 1923. Note the vee-fronted opening windscreen and the Ace wheel discs concealing the wire wheels. In October 1929 King George II of Greece became the car's second owner.*

ABOVE, AND RIGHT: *H.J. Mulliner's original six-light saloon with division on Phantom III chassis 3DL 102. There was a Perspex roof section just above the windscreen and the division glass dropped down out of sight when not required. Handbrake and gearlever were on the right of the driving seat in the usual Rolls-Royce position. These pictures show the car when in the King of Greece's ownership before it was rebodied.*

prudent to re-body one of the Phantom IIIs, thus saving money by not purchasing a complete new vehicle; the chassis chosen was 3 DL 102.

In January 1950, the Master of the Royal Household, Mr Averoff, called at Hooper's showrooms in St James', London, to discuss the possibility of re-bodying the Phantom as an open touring vehicle. Design 8276 was in many ways similar to the open tourer body on a Daimler Straight Eight chassis which had been completed for the British Royal Tour of South Africa. After consultation with the Tatoi Palace in Athens in early March, the decision was made to ship the Phantom back to the United Kingdom. When it arrived in mid-April, the condition of the chassis was such that

Rolls-Royce strongly suggested remedial action before any work commenced. Accordingly, the V-12 unit was decarbonised, valves renewed and noise from the tappets remedied. The clutch was relined, the steering slackness was taken up, the rear axle pinion thrust bearing replaced and, finally, the radiator matrix was worked on. Before Hooper & Co started their work, however, the complete chassis had to be rewired. Unfortunately, the bill was now already over budget and the Master of the Household announced that further work could not be paid for as the Royal Household simply did not hold enough funds in the United Kingdom. Eventually, the King stepped in and authorised the extra expenditure.

Hooper & Co made a start on the bodywork which was to be a four-door open type with a concealed hood. The specification also included: "…two 'H' pattern occasional facing forward seats, made to meet in the

The King of Greece's Hooper cabriolet body on 3DL 102 had a pair of wide forward-facing occasional seats to accommodate the royal children.

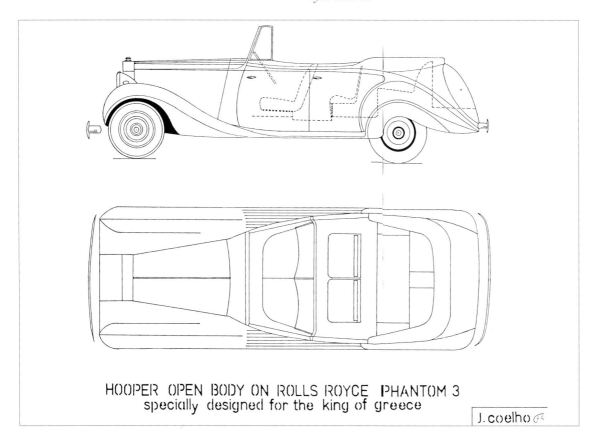

HOOPER OPEN BODY ON ROLLS ROYCE PHANTOM 3
specially designed for the king of greece

J. coelho

```
         H.M. The King of Greece - Hooper Open Trg. Body on
              40/50 Rolls-Royce Ph. III 3-DL-102.
```

Engine.

```
      Decarbonise the unit to the R.15 schedule of operations
      Renew valves, valve guides as necessary
      Remedy noise from the bottom tappets
      Recondition the water pump
      Adjust the oil pressure release valve
      Recondition and reset the carburettor
      Remedy water leaks from the cylinder head core plugs
      Remove heater connections
      Supply and fit high speed fan
      Renew the flywheel starter gear ring if found necessary
              on inspection
```

Clutch:
```
      Reline the unit.
```

Steering.
```
      Remove unit from the chassis, remedy excessive radial
           slackness.
```

Front Suspension
```
      Clean and adjust the cross and side steering tube joints
```

Brakes.
```
      Externally adjust all brakes and servo
```

Rear Axle.
```
      Balance the propeller shaft
      Renew the pinion thrust bearing
      Lubricate the wheel drivers.
```

Miscellaneous.
```
      Repair or renew the radiator matrix
      Test and adjust the centralized lubrication system
      Repair or replace the thermometer
      Repair the speedometer cable
      Correct the shock damper oil levels
      Renew the exhaust tail pipe and extend to suit the new body.
```

The complicated Rolls-Royce Phantom III chassis required some remedial work to bring it up to scratch. The high speed fan fitment and attention to the radiator matrix were no doubt to overcome cooling problems.

centre to carry three children." No division window was to be fitted, neither was a heater or radio. The existing front and rear wings were used from the old body, as were the rear wheel spats and wheeldiscs. The existing dashboard instruments, wing mirrors and bumpers were used where practicable. Heraldry was to be fitted in Athens, but detachable flagstaffs were fitted to both front wings. Specially selected black walnut woodwork was utilised and this complemented the Connolly red leather to the front

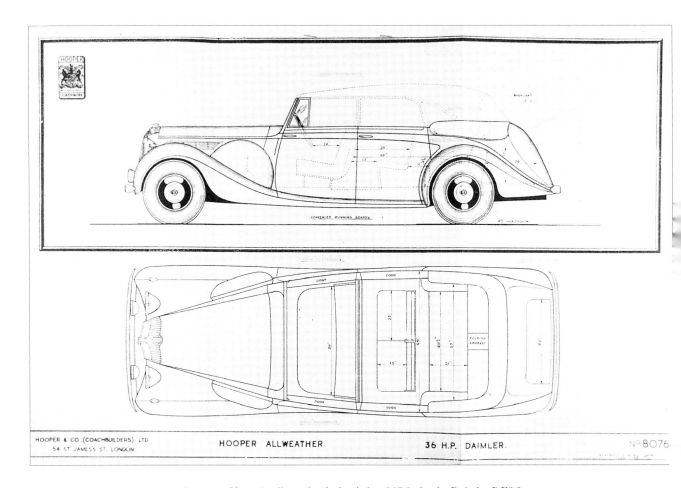

ABOVE: *Hooper's all-weather body, design 8076, for the Daimler DE36
Straight-Eight used for the 1947 Royal Tour of South Africa was in many
ways similar to the body built for the King of Greece's Phantom III.*
RIGHT: *In 1959 King Paul of Greece took delivery of this Silver Wraith
with Hooper body.*

and rear seats, which in the back sported a specially dyed red lambskin rug.
The colour for the finished Rolls-Royce was Hooper no.2 Blue all over (this
was a rather dark blue) and a red picking out line was added. A last minute
decision was made to to re-chromium plate the headlamps, bumpers and
wheel-discs. Nine months after its arrival at the coachbuilder's Western
Avenue factory, the completed open four-door tourer was finally ready. The
Rolls-Royce Phantom III was shipped to Greece in early March, 1951, just
in time to take part in a major parade scheduled for 25 March.

The Phantom III chassis was not a good performer in the heat, especially when serviced irregularly. In the summer months, Athens was pretty

unbearable and the Phantom III caused the driver considerable anxiety. Possibly the final straw was the harm sustained on a railway trip to the northern town of Thessalonika, when damage was sustained by the tourer rolling forward and hitting the wagon ends. The wings, radiator and head-lamps all needed attention; the R100 headlamps were replaced by those from a Packard. After this mishap, the car was withdrawn from regular use and eventually put up for auction in 1966. The new owner repaired the damaged parts and refitted a new set of Lucas headlamps; he also had the car repainted and replaced the hood. Since auction the car has only covered about 2,500 miles.

After years of acquiring used Rolls-Royce cars, King Paul decided to enquire whether Hooper & Co could design a brand new car for his needs.

The King of Greece's 1959 Silver Wraith, chassis LHLW 44, was fitted with a Hooper allweather body to design 8537. Note the very neat arrangement of the folded hood. A full-length detachable Perspex roof could be fitted.

Once again, His Majesty favoured a seven-seater open tourer. Curiously, at this time the Commonwealth of Australia had asked for drawings of a similar car, based on the lwb Silver Wraith chassis of 11ft 1in. In the end, however, only the centre sections of each car matched each other. The Monarch agreed to the accepted plan for an all-weather vehicle with a folding canvas head to which a Perspex top could be fitted over the passenger compartment. The cost was just on £6,000, less 20% to Rolls-Royce. Added to this, of course, was the cost of the chassis, which was just under £3,000. Again the King was keen to use the car for the March parade and requested delivery in time. For the first time, the chassis was to be left-hand-drive and the Hooper design chosen was 8537. Although a division was fitted across the car, there was no window actually installed. An all-metal aluminium construction was used with accommodation for two on the front seat, two on the rear seat and two on occasional seats which met in the centre. The front- and rear-hinged doors had manual windows and the canvas

OFR/EGM   10th March   59

Messrs. Rolls-Royce Ltd.,
Export Department,
14-15 Conduit Street,
London W.1.

<u>For the attention of Mr. B.A. Vatier</u>

Dear Sirs,

                    H.M. The King of Greece
            <u>Hooper Allweather on Silver Wraith LHLW.44</u>

        With reference to the transparent Perspex top
fitted to the above car, the two enclosed photographs
Nos. 58823 and 4 have been specially taken to
demonstrate how the Perspex roof should be supported
when being removed or placed in position in order to
avoid undue distortion and possible fracture.

        It will be observed that there should be four
men, one at each corner with a fifth man inside the
car ready to ease the roof on or off.

        Would you also advise the person or persons
concerned that if the Perspex roof is removed and
put in storage, then it should be supported on wooden
trestles say, three in number, the top of the trestles
being approximately to the curvature of the roof and
covered with soft cloth over thick felt. This form of
support will prevent damage and distortion and a light
dust cover placed over the roof will exclude dust and
avoid the possibility of scatching when the roof is
cleaned.

                                          contd.

                         -2-

        Special polish and polishing cloths were sent
with the car for polishing the Perspex top. It is
most important that this polish <u>ONLY</u> is used for
that purpose; any other substance is liable to
damage the Perspex. Further supplies can be obtained
from us when the present supply is exhausted.

        Trusting that this information will be of use,

                         Yours faithfully,
              HOOPER & CO. (Coachbuilders) LIMITED.

                              Director
                              & Chief Designer

Enc.

*The 1959 Silver Wraith Hooper allweather was also used by King
Constantine II who succeeded to the Greek throne in 1964.*

spring-assisted head folded back and a matching cover could be fitted.
The complicated Perspex top extended from the top screen rail to the back
rail and enveloped the hood recess. Triplex were to build it to a former
design supplied by Hooper & Co. The transparent top, which cost £1,000,
was to be made easily detachable without overlooking the fact that five men
were required to remove it safely. Hooper's instructions were clear that the
Perspex top should be supported throughout its length when being installed
or removed, otherwise it might well fracture. They advised: "…there should
be four men, one at each corner, with a fifth man inside the car ready to
ease the roof on or off." This time heaters, demisters and a medium wave
radio with electric aerial were installed. The back seat incorporated a centre folding armrest in which was fitted a covered leather-lined tray. Separate
switches could activate the interior lighting fitted above the twin loud-

speakers fitted into the back of the windowless division. Once again the vehicle was finished in Hooper No. 2 blue with a red picking out line. The interior was identical to the previous tourer too, with the exception of the rear seat rug which was nylon. The front and rear seats were provided by Connolly Bros. Finally, a flagstaff was ordered to be fitted to the right hand mudguard. The order was confirmed in the middle of July and the chassis, numbered LHLW 44, was delivered for the bodywork on 29 August. Progress continued on the ceremonial car over the next five months and it was completed in plenty of time for the March parade. On the 6th of that month, the car was handed over to the shippers.

However, there was one mishap. Hooper & Co had arranged for the heraldic painter G.C. Francis to apply his skills to the main doors, but initially he was busy on Royal Tour work and delayed starting. A week later he had flu and soon after that broke his right wrist. When the transfers arrived in Athens on 24 March, nobody could fix them to the car. In desperation, Mr Coutroubis (the Athens distributor) organised a very temporary arrangement. Hooper & Co were quick to apologise and explain Mr Francis's misfortunes, but added darkly: "we have taken this matter up very strongly with Mr Francis and have gone as far as contemplating putting some of our heraldic work elsewhere." I am happy to say that Mr

The hood was lowered before the Perspex roof could be fitted on the 1959 Silver Wraith, a potentially hazardous operation; given the length of the roof, there was always the possibility that it would fracture.

Francis is still working and at the time of writing is into his 85th year.

The final car to be delivered to the Hellenic household was in the first month of 1965, a year after the death of King Paul. The customer was the new King Constantine, who was to have only a short reign after the military coup against the Civil Government in 1967. Risking his life, the King staged a counter-coup, but this failed and he and his family were forced to flee to Italy. However, during his reign, His Majesty received a Silver Cloud III Mulliner Park Ward drophead coupé (modified from the standard steel saloon) with the chassis number LSHS 329C. This was, generally speaking, a recreational vehicle – design 2007 – with just two doors and four seats. It is unlikely to have been used on State occasions, as the more suitable Silver Wraith tourer was already in the palace garage.

What was the ultimate fate of the Rolls-Royce cars? The Phantom III limousine was reported by the British Embassy to be kept 'somewhere' in Greece. The other Phantom III open tourer went to a Greek enthusiast who later had his car impounded by anti-monarchists. This was also the fate of the 1959 Silver Wraith, although I believe that this car is still kept at Tatoi. The Government's explanation is that it does not recognise Royal ownership, and that the Greek Republic owns them as State property.

Ireland

The Republic of Ireland ordered a State landaulette on a Rolls-Royce chassis which, when completed, was certainly the most expensive car ever acquired by the authorities in Eire. Initially the Republic favoured an open tourer but later abandoned the idea when it was pointed out that, whereas a Daimler Straight Eight chassis could accommodate such a size on a wheelbase of 12ft 3ins, it was plainly impracticable on the then largest Rolls-Royce chassis which was only 10ft 7ins. With an electric division and two occasional seats there would be hardly any boot. On 21 January 1949, Hooper & Co were told by Jack Scott of Rolls-Royce that the new State car was to come through the coachbuilders as a landaulette. Chief designer Osmond Rivers submitted design 8178 which was altered only very slightly. A curved glass Triplex panel was set into the roof to allow more natural light into the rear; it was operated by an electric shutter. There was also a dictaphone to convey the wishes of the rear seat to the driver. Hooper also arranged for the rear seat to be altered by forward and rear peg adjustment. A hand mirror was to be fitted into a slot in the offside elbow rest, a silk blind to the division window when privacy was required and there was space on the back of the division for a loudspeaker grille and heater outlet. Rolls-Royce at Crewe allocated chassis WGC 1 and it arrived on 26 May.

The order for the new State car had been handled by one of the directors of Dublin's oldest Rolls-Royce distributor, Huet Motors. A month after the chassis was delivered to Western Avenue for the bodywork, Mr Huet arrived. It was pointed out that there had been some 'slippage', mostly caused by the indecision over the coachwork. However, he quite understood and the only alteration was to change the coachline to Shamrock green. As the car was being painted in Hooper no.2 blue, this made a distinctive contrast and it is likely that the head leather was dyed to match.

The rear seating caused some concern because the new President had recently tried a Humber Pullman limousine and had found the seats particularly comfortable. The coachbuilders obtained a copy of a Humber catalogue, but in the meantime a new Humber came in to Hoopers for attention and measurements were taken. The new President was not a tall man and this problem was resolved by the provision of two removable

ST.JAMES'S STREET.   HF/ES   28th June 1949.

PRESIDENT OF EIRE.

9561 "Hooper" Landaulette on
Silver Wraith chassis WCC-1.

Mr.Huet called at the works and inspected the above
car. We told him that we expected to have the car ready
for delivery about the early part of September, and in answer
to a question by him said that it was impossible to finish
it by the 5th August. The reason for the delay, as he suggested,
was the fact that the Authorities in Ireland had delayed the
original order so long.

Left pattern of paint which was handed to Mr.Rivers.
This is very similar to No.2 blue, but made up by Mr.Huet
himself. He has part of the panel for comparison when the
car is finished.   Shamrock green picking-out line on mouldings.

Left also samples of dark blue leather for the trimming
of the front compartment; grey Bedford cord for the main
compartment, and plain 62 grey cloth for the headlining.
Duplicates of these are on St.James's Street file and also
on Mr.Huet's file.   Samples handed to Mr.Stiff - foreman
trimmer.

The trimming to the front seat is to be the standard
pleated style, and the main compartment our standard plain
style.

The President has already sat in an ordinary new Humber
Pullman and finds the angle, depth and height of this
particular car rather comfortable for normal travelling.
We will obtain a catalogue from Humbers and let you have details
The two loose overlay cushions are to be fitted in addition
so that for ceremonial journeys the President can sit on one
and be more in view of the populous. (He is a short man,
approximately 5'6" in height, though his wife is rather tall).

Walnut flame veneer woodwork left to our discretion.

It was decided that the automatic door switches could be
left off and normal switches fitted for the roof lights of the
main compartment in the front end of the armrests. These can
be wired direct to the accumulator and not through the master
switch.

The Presidential flag will be worn on both sides of the
car, and although 2 masts xxxxxxxxxxxxxxxxxx were required
fitted just aft of the headlamps, we finally persuaded Mr.Huet
that the most convenient place was in the centre of both wings.
The lower edge of the flag is to fly about level with the
radiator cap, or top line of the bonnet, provided this does not
mean that the mast is not too high. The mast is to be made
detachable and a small milled screw-in blemish plate is to be
supplied when the mast is not in use.

Very important. Our name-plates advertising "Hooper" coachwork are not to have any reference to our Royal family, or to
the effect that we are coachbuilders by Royal Warrant of
Appointment. Mr.Huet agrees that this is a point that
probably does not matter, but if any of their local rag press
got hold of our name-plates they would make a very big story
out of it.   It is the first British car that has been bought
officially by the country, and he hopes to get much further
business from it.   He had to overcome a lot of opposition and
criticism.

A Hooper memo of 28 June 1949 goes into considerable detail concerning the interior fitments for the President of Eire's Silver Wraith landaulette and ends with an important political note.

CALLS INSTRUCTION.   9561

HOOPER & CO. (Coachbuilders)LTD. | Job No.

Contractor. Huet Motors   Contractor's Order No.
Customer   President of Eire   Customer's Order No.

One   Landaulette   Body to Design   8178 | Body No 9561

For   RR.S.Wraith   Chassis No.

Delivery Reqd.   Delivery Scheduled

To Specification No.   Body Price   Amendments
                                                          & Dates

Colour Scheme:-

        Dark Blue all over exactly as approved pattern.

     Picking out line in shamrock green.

Trim Details:-
        Front seat in Connolly's Dark Blue leather VM.8090.
        Rear compartment - Grey Bedford Cord 1148
        Headlining   Playnes grey 62.
        Style   Plain style to the rear;
                           Pleated style to the front.
        Carpet   Blue 90851 to front and boot
                           Grey to rear to be decided. AP349.

Interior Woodwork:-   Walnut flame veneer.

Variations from Standard Specification:-

1. The automatic door switches NOT to be fitted. Switches for the roof
   lamps to be positioned in the front end of the armrests.
2. Rear seat to be similar to the Humber Pullman.
3. Two loose overlay cushions to be fitted to the rear seat.
4. Two flagstaffs, socket on centre of each front wing. Flagstaff to
   be made by H & Co. to special drawing.
5. 'Hooper' name plates to be fitted WITHOUT reference to our Royal
   Family or Royal Warrant.

Issued by   Date   Sanctioned by   Date
        PGM   1.7.49.
                                     Managing Director

ABOVE: *Hooper's works instruction for the building of body no. 9561
giving colour and trim details plus special requirements.*
RIGHT: *The Hooper drawing of design 8178 showing the principal
dimensions.*

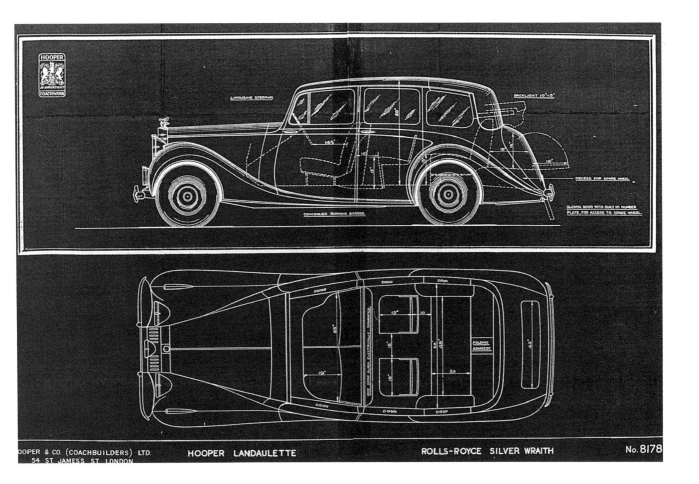

cushions each of which were about two-and-a-half inches in depth.

At one time Dublin had wanted the Republic's new flag to be positioned to the near and offside front bumper, with a mast tall enough to clear the large P100 Lucas headlamps. Eventually Hoopers convinced the authorities that a more convenient place would be the centre of both front wings, where they could easily be removed and the space filled by screw-in blemish covers. The switch which automatically turned on the interior lights was omitted from the rear doors, and a manual switch was now fitted to the front end of the armrests.

The recent departure of Ireland from the British Commonwealth made the sale politically sensitive and this was reflected in a memo from Hooper's sales manager at St. James's: "Very important; our name plates advertising Hooper coachwork are not to have any references to our Royal Family or to the effect that we are coachbuilders by Royal Warrant of

Appointment. It is the first British car to be bought officially by the country." Probably by coincidence, Hooper & Co did omit all references to the British monarchy from their sill nameplates on all the vehicles which they built thereafter.

A decision about the rear seat material was reached, and it was to be a grey ribbed cloth with the front seat furnished in dark blue leather. Shortly after the upholstery was decided on, the flag of the Irish Republic arrived and Osmond Rivers tried out the new scheme for flying the flag from the wing, which was satisfactory.

On 21 September, some fifteen months after a State car was first mooted, the Rolls-Royce Silver Wraith was handed over for shipment to Ireland's capital. From then on the car was in the charge of the Department of Defence, until 1973 when it was passed to the Irish police, Garda Siochana. In the intervening years it has become a part of the nation's pageantry and makes appearances at all major functions involving the President and State visitors. It has conveyed President Kennedy, the King and Queen of Belgium, the Prince of Monaco and many important church leaders. Such an active life led to a decision to refurbish the car in 1977. This entailed stripping the paint, beating out some panels and then

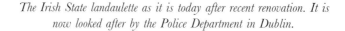

The Irish State landaulette as it is today after recent renovation. It is now looked after by the Police Department in Dublin.

Eire's President, Patrick J. Hillery, drives through the streets of Dublin in the Hooper Silver Wraith on the way to his inauguration for his second term of office in 1983. The special flag masts are used on such occasions.

repainting the car completely. The wood was repolished and the upholstery attended to. Mechanically, the engine was overhauled and this included fitting a reconditioned crankshaft vibration damper and attending to various other minor details. Rolls-Royce material was used throughout. With a mileage of around 90,000m, Ireland's premier State car still has many years of playing a leading role in Ireland's presidential life ahead of it. To date, it is the only Rolls-Royce State car delivered to the Republic.

THE NETHERLANDS

The House of Orange has only had one State Rolls-Royce since the Second World War. It is, however, true that HRH Prince Bernhard did enjoy Bentleys and for some time used them on private journeys. HM Queen Juliana placed an order with Rolls-Royce for a suitable State car in the summer of 1957. The body style chosen was a landaulette. The wholly-owned coachbuilding subsidiary of Rolls-Royce was Park Ward who had already been chosen by their holding company to build five landaulettes for State use based on their standard limousine introduced in late 1955. Oddly, all the Park Ward-built landaulettes went to Africa. One should bear in mind that until the mid-fifties, State cars for the Colonies and Governor-Generals had been built by a variety of coach-builders, with Hooper & H.J. Mulliner predominating. In the late fifties, however, there was a policy decision to switch entirely to Park Ward for Government orders, apart from two Hooper landaulettes. Park Ward had been founded in the twenties and had perfected a system to produce all metal bodies by the end of the thirties, firstly on Bentley and latterly on a handful of Rolls-Royce Wraiths. After the war, Park Ward used all-metal construction only, and the hardiness of their saloons, dropheads and limousines convinced many other coach-builders to adopt a similar method – Hooper in 1949 and H.J. Mulliner on a regular basis from 1953.

Chassis LGLW 24 was the only Park Ward landaulette for State use delivered with left-hand steering. The car was painted black with a gold picking-out line added along the sides. The car colour matched the black enamelled Connolly leather roof, which of course folded down from the rear standing pillar. Beige leather front seating was complemented by light grey cloth in the rear. Initially, the usual Radiomobile receiver 4220 was planned, but in the event a special set was fitted into the rear left armrest, which was a unique model manufactured by Philips of Eindhoven, who placed a miniature crown on the face of the set. The matching armrest containeded a mirror, notebook, and cigarette case plus heater and division

RIGHT: *The 1958 Silver Wraith Park Ward landaulette, design no 727, delivered to Queen Juliana of the Netherlands, was really a variation on the standard Park Ward limousine, which it effectively became when the car was closed.*

Queen Juliana of the Netherlands, accompanied by her husband Prince Bernhard, alights from the Silver Wraith Park Ward landaulette, LGLW 24. Its design was well suited to use on formal occasions.

controls. To the rear of the division opposite the rear seat occupants, a cabinet was installed which contained two decanters and four tumblers. On the peaks of both front wings were fitted detachable flag masts which were placed ahead of the two mirrors. All of the windows, including the rear quarter-lights, were manually operated. The State landaulette was sent for testing on 26 February 1958 and sailed for The Hook of Holland on the *Amsterdam,* just over two weeks later and the guarantee card was issued on 13 March. The cost to the Dutch Royal Household was close to £9,000. On arrival, the car received a monogrammed 'J' surmounted by a crown on both main rear doors.

The Rolls-Royce remained at the Royal Palace for twenty years and conveyed a number of important passengers, including Queen Elizabeth II, the Shah of Iran, the King of Thailand and King Olaf, as well as many of the world's leaders and presidents. In this time, the car had covered a mere 45,000 miles and covered virtually no distance in the last two or three years, but this situation was soon to change. Suddenly in the autumn of 1978, The Queen decided to set a public example and dispose of her less than fuel efficient Silver Wraith. (One should bear in mind that Her Majesty was reputed to be one of the world's wealthiest women and also possessed a substantial holding in Royal Dutch Shell…) Early in the New Year the landaulette was acquired privately and has often travelled over much of Northern Europe to rallies and other events. At the time of writing, the only major incidents appeared to be the necessity to renew the automatic gearbox and attend to the rear compartment cloth upholstery and renew the front leather seats. The car is now in its third ownership and has been with its latest Dutch owner since 1984.

POLAND

The political situation in Poland is one that has often fascinated or confounded historians. Indeed it was a country that virtually disappeared from the end of the 18th century until its reconstitution after the Great War in 1918. Between the First and Second World Wars, two very eminent individuals could claim to have been Head of State and both chose Rolls-Royce motor cars for their progress. Josef Pilsudski was actually proclaimed Chief of State in 1918, but turned down the offer of the Presidency in 1922. However, in 1926 he brought about what was in effect a *coup d'etat* and became President in all but name, directing both the military and exercising enormous influence in foreign policy, despite vigorous opposition from the Polish Parliament. When he died in 1935 his past eccentricities were glossed over and he received a State funeral.

Marshal Pilsudski ordered an lhd Phantom II Rolls-Royce in early 1932. This was chassis 223 AMS and for its coachwork the chassis was sent to Barker & Co. The choice was an all-weather tourer with twin mounted spare tyres to either side of the front wing and a scuttle-mounted spotlight which was almost as large as the car's headlamps. These, plus the 'loudest possible horns', certainly gave the open car a certain presence. In anticipation of a change of specification, 223 AMS was fitted with a 28 gallon fuel tank with 6 gallons in reserve. At this time the normal capacity was a mere 20 gallons. The eminent military man obviously feared that Polish roads would do their worst and wisely ordered four spare front springs. Delivery was made to the Rolls-Royce representative in Warsaw, Count Andrew Tarnowski, and the guarantee became effective from 28 November 1932. What has happened to this tourer is not known but it is unlikely to have survived the Second World War.

Wladyslaw Sikorski was certainly opposed to Pilsudski's dictatorship and, after only two years as Prime Minister, retired from active life in the mid-twenties. When war became inevitable, he offered his services, but no response was forthcoming. Rolls-Royce came into General Sikorski's life in the late thirties, when an order was placed for a Phantom III chassis. Oddly enough, the coachbuilder chosen was Vanvooren of Paris, who constructed excellent bodies in the twenties and thirties. Chassis 3 CM81 was a rather dashing two-seater drophead coupé which, for its time, sported the rather *demodé* split windscreen. Again two side-mounted spares were fitted, but in this case they were protected from the elements by aluminium covers. The windscreen's scuttle-mounted spotlamps were capable of being swivelled through an arc. Should the front opening doors show any inclination to drop, they were supported by three massive hinges. Rather unusually, the rear spats could be worn either on the vehicle or without. The completed drophead was transported to Warsaw and the guarantee was issued in April 1938 for three years. It is rumoured that when Poland was invaded and the country's fate essentially sealed – yet another convulsion in that country's turbulent history – General Sikorski loaded the car up and fled westward.

The car was still in his possession in 1943 when he died in an aircraft attempting to take off from Gibraltar airfield. Chassis 3 CM 81 remained as part of his estate until the early fifties and is now resident in the United States.

PORTUGAL

The Government of Portugal has owned only one Rolls-Royce, although it does make use of a Phantom III cabriolet, which is called in whenever an open car is required. The latter vehicle started life as one of India's more exotic acquisitions. Prince Berar of Hydrabad had ordered it in the early summer of 1937 and the coachbuilders Windovers made what has remained a unique car with a Lalique radiator-mounted mascot whose colouring could be changed from red to blue. The car also sported sunken door handles, inset foglamps, purdah glass, toilet requisites, ice-box, solid silver Thermos flask and even an auto-change record player in the boot which could be operated from the dash. To warn of the car's approach, six horns were mounted on the apron in front of the radiator. A side-mounted spare wheel was also supplied, as were a set of Marchal headlamps and an extra set of lamps to either side of the windscreen. The finished colour scheme was mustard and maroon and the car was shipped to India in February 1938. Chassis 3CP 116 remained in the sub-continent until it returned to Britain in about 1953.

The then owner, a Captain Radcliffe, who knew of the Queen's forthcoming State visit to Portugal, arranged for the Phantom to receive coachwork modifications at Hooper & Co. The car arrived in the autumn of 1956 and much work had to be carried out. The multi-coloured mascot went, as did the side-mounted spare wheel, built in foglamps, six horns, low-fitted rear wheelspats, windscreen-mounted lamps and triple-barred front and rear bumpers. The car was repainted black with a gold picking-out line and the more usual twin horns and twin sidelights adapted. A radiator-mounted flagmast was acquired as well as the facility to fly standards from either of the front wings. The interior also received attention and the car was in place for The Queen's visit in February 1957. The cabriolet was subsequently taken over by the Republican Presidency of Portugal. Her Majesty used the

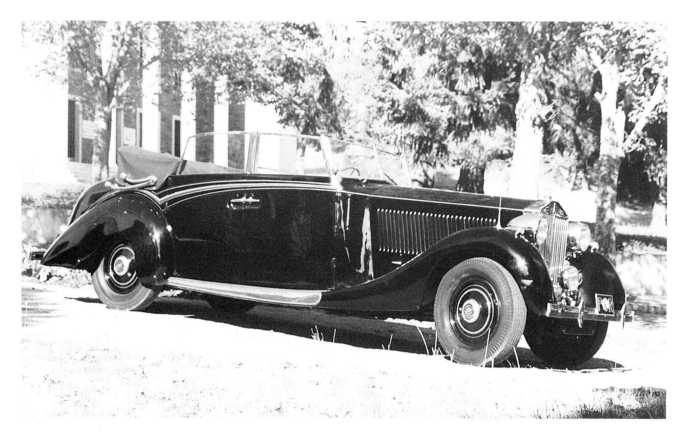

ABOVE, AND BELOW: *This Phantom III, chassis 3CP 116, started life as a Windovers cabriolet for Prince Berar. In 1956 Hooper modified it slightly for use by Queen Elizabeth II on a state visit to Portugal in 1957.*

car again during her second State visit in 1985. The vehicle has also been loaned for other national events, including President Eisenhower's visit and those of two of the more recent Popes. Since 1978, the Windovers/Hooper cabriolet has been housed at the Museu do Caramuloin in Northern Portugal and was still available for visiting dignitaries until recently.

The first brand-new Rolls-Royce purchased for the use of the President of Portugal was a Park Ward bodied lhd Phantom V. The order was placed in the spring of 1960 on chassis 5LAT 84 and was virtually a standard

Coachbuilders drawing showing the main dimensions of the Park Ward limousine, design number. 980, on the Phantom V chassis as supplied to the President of Portugal in 1960 (chassis 5LAT 84). Still at work in its fourth decade.

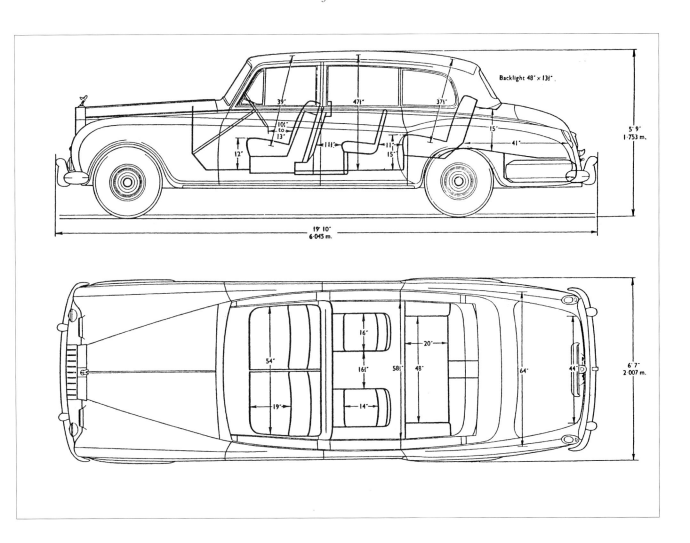

provisioned car which had: speedometer in kilometres, high frequency horns, rear compartment radio (which was of the hybrid variety – half valve and half transistor), a cabinet behind the division with two decanters and four glasses, cigarette case, notebook, mirror and wool rug in front of the rear seat. Park Ward sent the completed car to be tested on 20 September and three weeks later it was shipped to Portugal where the guarantee came into operation in October 1960. Since then, the black-painted Phantom V has remained with the Presidency of the Republic of Portugal and often makes appearances at visits by foreign Heads of State.

Romania

Romania was a Monarchy from 1866 until it became a Republic in the final month of 1947. However, there seems now to be a possibility that the monarchy could be restored. From 1965, the main influence was the dictator Nicolae Ceausescu who became President in 1967 and ruled until his overthrow and subsequent execution in December 1989. From the 1920s until the late 1960s, Romania offered a strong market for Head of State transport.

After the First World War, King Ferdinand and his somewhat eccentric consort Queen Marie occupied the throne and ordered a pair of Rolls-Royce 40/50hp Silver Ghosts in 1919. As one was a closed limousine and the other an open torpedo tourer, it is unlikely that they were used individually by the King and Queen, and in many ways it would not be unreasonable to assume that from time to time they would share the Ghosts. The King's car was a fully enclosed limousine with a side-mounted spare wheel, blinds to the rear compartment windows and a scuttle-mounted flashlight. Emblazoned on the rear doors was the King's emblem which was, in all likelihood, painted by one of the Francis family, who had already cornered the market in heraldic decoration. The Queen's car was an open tourer of decidedly racy appearance, which probably reflected her outré temperament. (Her Majesty was inclined to leave *billet doux* around the Palace saying how beautiful she was – and in her teens she assuredly had been – until she was well into her fifties). Both Silver Ghosts had been bodied by the

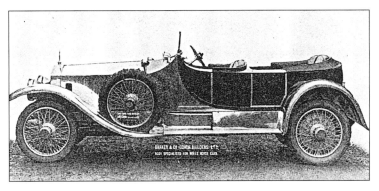

TOP: *40/50hp Barker limousine supplied to King Ferdinand of Romania
was complete with a luggage grid at the rear.*
ABOVE: *40/50hp Barker torpedo tourer supplied to Queen Marie of
Romania had very rakish lines.*

London coachbuilder Barker & Co. Presumably the Rolls-Royces were shipped to Bucharest and garaged in the Royal castle of Sinaia. It is entirely possible that both vehicles put in an appearance at the wedding of the couple's daughter in June 1922. This was followed four months later by the second Coronation of the King and Queen; this time of a greater Romania much enlarged at the expense of Hungary which had lost territory in the Great War.

The next Rolls-Royce state vehicles to be purchased were by King Carol II and both were mighty V-12 Phantom IIIs. Carol II (who had as much eccentricity in him as his mother and a private life which kept a generation highly intrigued), placed an order for one of the first sanction of chassis, the AZ series, at the end of March 1936. The King requested a two seater drophead coupé from Gurney Nutting, the one time coachbuilders to the then Prince of Wales, on chassis 3AZ 50. Its designer was the famed A.F. McNeil, who was later to design for James Young. The Phantom was possibly the most beautiful of its kind to emerge and it really looked very sleek. The car was fitted at the rear with a detachable luggage boot which certainly complemented the line of the coachwork, as did the pram-iron roof supports. To cope with the climatic conditions in Romania, Rolls-Royce ensured that the bonnet louvres were full length and ran into the scuttle. Although the photograph shows a break in the line of the 'b' post, indicating a full convertible and not a sedanca coupé, it does show that an electric back light blind was included, as indeed was a dummy hub wheel-carrier. The car was painted dark blue with a grey top and the completed vehicle went off for test on 27 June. It was handed over to the King in the second week of September 1936.

In May 1937, King George VI was crowned in great splendour at Westminster Abbey and later played host to King Carol II at a State Banquet. At the same time, Jack Barclay had just taken into stock a Park Ward-bodied touring limousine which, to all intents, looked very similar to the razor edge design much employed by H.J. Mulliner. This was on Phantom III chassis 3CP 34, which had been tested in May. An electric division and back light were fitted and the car emerged painted in

King Carol II of Romania took delivery of this Phantom III V-12, chassis 3AZ 50, in 1936. It was fitted with this elegant Owen Sedanca Drophead Coupé body built by Gurney Nutting to the design of London car dealers H.R. Owen.

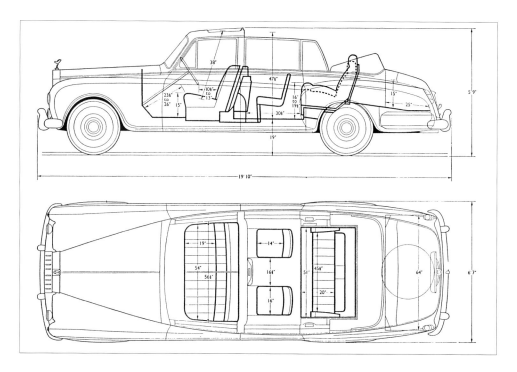

H.J. Mulliner, Park Ward drawing showing the dimensions and layout of the ceremonial State Landaulette, design 2052, on the Phantom V chassis.

contrasting shades with the top colour the lighter of the two. The vehicle was handed over to the owner at the end of July 1937 and it is likely that delivery was taken in London. In September 1940, the Balkan monarch was forced to abdicate and was succeeded by the nineteen-year-old King Michael, who reigned for just under seven years until a communist government was installed by the Russians. The fate of the two Phantom IIIs is not known; certainly the beautiful Gurney Nutting drophead disappeared, but the Park Ward touring limousine survived the Second World War and was sold in 1948 to a Romanian buyer.

The next purchase of a Rolls-Royce led to a most bizarre set of circumstances. In late 1966, Mulliner Park Ward received an order to build a State landaulette to their design 2052, which had been introduced in 1965 and was based on the Phantom V model. Chassis 5LVF 113 had a power-operated hood which closed just behind the driver's compartment, power-adjustable rear seats and a host of extras, including a refrigerated wine cooler. The total cost made it the most expensive State landaulette at the time. At just under £20,000, then a huge sum, it was almost double the cost

The ex-Romanian Phantom V Mulliner Park Ward State Landaulette, chassis 5LVF 113, when owned by Dr Erle M. Heath. It was originally delivered to the Romanian Embassy in London on 8th April 1967 and registered NLD 39E. This was the fourth of only five of these special State Landaulettes built on the Phantom V chassis.

of a standard Phantom V. In March 1967 Rolls-Royce sent a note to Bucharest saying that the car would be ready for collection in about three weeks. However, the government tried to rescind the order almost at once, despite having paid for the vehicle. It was thought that a question had been raised in the Romanian Parliament about the ordering of one of capitalism's most potent symbols. Eventually, faced with the fact that the Rolls-Royce company would not co-operate, the Romanian government accepted the landaulette which was shipped first to Geneva and then on to Bucharest. However, they were determined not to use the car and even the State visit of General de Gaulle did not bring the Rolls-Royce out of its hiding-place.

In between times, the State Landaulette ran up some 1,500 miles but, after a year, Rolls-Royce were asked to exchange the Phantom for a less opulent model. Although a Silver Shadow was mooted, it is not known whether this car ended up in Bucharest or was used solely by the Romanian ambassador to Britain.

The Phantom V State landaulette was taken back and a new owner was found in the United States, a Dr Heath from Pennsylvania. The car is again up for sale following his death. The car has covered some 117,000 miles and has twice been borrowed by Her Majesty The Queen for visits to the Cayman Islands, and later Bermuda. So the Phantom was used as intended, for a Head of State, after all.

SPAIN

During the early years of this century, the Spanish Head of State, King Alfonso XIII, was known to be an enthusiastic car owner who occasionally drove himself – reportedly at around 75mph. Hispano-Suiza, at that time based in Spain, supplied many of the grandees with their transport, although the British Daimler company was responsible for quite a few limousines and landaulettes up until the departure of the speed-enthusiast monarch in 1931. This was followed by a period of civil unrest, then the Civil War, from which General Franco emerged triumphant in 1939.

The first Rolls-Royce came in 1948, when a Silver Wraith sedanca de ville, chassis WCB 17, with H.J. Mulliner coachwork was ordered through Don Carlos de Salamanca, the Rolls-Royce Spanish distributor. This car had been at the 1948 Earls Court exhibition and was painted maroon (later changed to black) with front seats in dark leather and rear compartment cloth in grey. The car was initially under the organisation of the Director-General of Military Transport in Madrid. It had been fitted with a kilometre speedometer, double filament headlamps, a separate switch on the instrument board for the centre light and was complete with locks to the petrol filler cap and bonnet. The Earls Court exhibit was the first of a new design, numbered 7055, which was to be a popular model, with quite a few being ordered by the British Ministry of Supply for use at overseas diplomatic stations. Chassis WCB 17 was used much more by the wife of General Franco, although whether this was because it was not armourplated is now hard to establish. The Silver Wraith was issued with its guarantee card on 15 January 1949 and to date has remained with the Spanish Head of State. Nowadays this 1948 car is no longer in use.

In 1948, the then Princess Elizabeth and The Duke of Edinburgh had ordered the first of what ultimately turned out to be the rare Phantom IV chassis. Rolls-Royce were not at first keen to build other chassis of this type, but when an order backed by the Foreign Office for three armour-plated cars was received in 1948, it was felt that the extra weight could, to some extent, be nullified by the more powerful 5,675cc straight-eight engine as opposed to the normal post-war 4 ¼ litre, six-cylinder unit. To this end, a development vehicle was constructed and used as a works delivery and test vehicle. In its ultimate development, with the B81 6,515cc engine and automatic transmission, this somewhat speedy truck was up before the local constabulary fairly frequently for exceeding 90mph, especially as the limit imposed on goods vehicles was only 30mph! It was dismantled in December 1963. As a matter of interest, the first four chassis were assembled at Belper, near Derby, where most of the experimental work was done, and the later chassis came from Crewe.

The Spanish Phantoms (now designated Phantom IV) were delivered in 1952 in the 'wrong' order; chassis 4AF 18 in March, 4AF 14 in June and 4AF 16 in July. Chassis 4AF 14 and 4AF16 were despatched to the coach-builders H.J. Mulliner on 2 March 1951, followed by 4AF 18 on 3 April 1951. The latter was to their cabriolet design 7183. As the car would possibly be used in dusty conditions it (along with the other two) was fitted with an oil-bath air cleaner. The cabriolet was fitted with protective armour up to waist level. More prosaically, it was fitted with special steering, a 4200 Radiomobile receiving set with adaptations, petrol gauge in litres, speedometer in kilometres and, again, an instrument board switch for the centre lamp. Painted black, it had green leather upholstery throughout. General Franco used this Phantom the least, possibly because of the risk to his life. It certainly appeared at most parades, but was rumoured to have only run up about 20,000 miles by the mid-eighties. Perhaps this was due to the fact that only one avenue in Madrid was considered to be safe enough for the Caudillo, as it was so wide that the high side of the folded hood (presumably with protection) gave any possible assailant too much of a problem with sight lines. Although still roadworthy, the cabriolet is rarely, if ever, seen on duty.

The two remaining Phantom IVs were of design 7181 and were similar in appearance. Chassis 4AF 14 was basically a four-seater but with no extra seats and a substantial floor to waist console between the main

ABOVE, AND FOLLOWING PAGES: *General Franco's Phantom IV*
H.J. Mulliner four-door cabriolet on chassis 4AF 18 was the first of
the trio of cars to be delivered in March 1952. It has special
American-type bumpers, flashing indicator lamps built into the front
wings and a second foglamp mounted above the bumper.

seats. Chassis 4AF 16, however, was described as a seven-seater and was presumably equipped with forward-facing seats which folded into the division when not required. Both cars had a single side-mounted spare wheel, (the cabriolet also had one on the nearside) and the radio had an aerial above the centre portion of the roof. Matching flag masts were fitted to both front wings. Both Phantoms were fitted with leather to front and cloth to rear, and also in the specification was an electrically-operated rear blind and division. Cross-banded walnut veneered woodwork in the division housed a heater, loudspeaker, lockable compartments and fold-down picnic tables, whilst reading lights and controls were fitted to either side of the main seat. Again, both cars were painted black. The armoured protection of all the Phantom IV cars caused considerable trouble and H.J. Mulliner (who were responsible for the coachwork) submitted metal samples as a matter of course to the Spanish military for testing against possible gunshots, but to everyone's chagrin the metal was easily penetrated. Fortunately, the

*1948 Silver Wraith Sedanca (chassis WCB 17) and 1952 Phantom IV
cabriolet (chassis 4AF 18) at the Palacio El Prado, Madrid. Both had
H.J. Mulliner bodies, the Silver Wraith's on a 127-inch wheelbase and the
Phantom IVs on a 145 inch wheelbase.*

Spaniards had also sent a sample of a material that was found to be resistant to bullets, and eventually English Steel and Triplex glass came up with a suitable replacement, immune even to the assault of high velocity rifles such as the Mauser. Curiously, the protection was only arranged around the rear compartments of the cars. The weight of the body alone on the limousines was a staggering one and a quarter tons.

It is well known that all the Phantoms are in occasional use and for some time they have been housed at Madrid's Palacio El Prado under the supervision of the Royal Guard. Maintenance has been done on a regular basis. Rolls-Royce changed the front suspension springs in August 1967 and an engineer from Crewe has visited from time to time, but the cars are normally serviced in Madrid these days.

One visiting Rolls-Royce man was quite surprised to see how little mileage the cars had on their speedometers and it was explained that, generally, the Phantoms were moved around by rail. General Franco lived a very public life and tight security was clearly necessary. It was strongly rumoured that the reason he had two identical cars was that both would

General Franco's two Phantom IV H.J. Mulliner limousines are now the property of King Juan Carlos and are still used by the Spanish royal family.

leave the Zarzuela Palace at similar times with a decoy general seated in one of them.

Today King Juan Carlos, Queen Sofia and the heir to the Spanish throne, Prince Felipe, occasionally use the cars which tend to be reserved for visits by other Heads of State. These certainly add to the pageantry and colour of the country's capital.

YUGOSLAVIA

Yugoslavia was proclaimed a Republic in November 1945 and had previously been a monarchy. The Yugoslav Royal Family had put its faith in the splendid American Packard. However, the story of the country's involvement with Rolls-Royce is really that of its most memorable leader, President Tito. In the thirty-five years that he ruled Yugoslavia until his death in 1980, he kept an iron hold on the Republic which, with Yugoslavia's present misfortune in mind, at least maintained peace. A communist state was imposed in 1946 and lasted until 1990, when the country gradually slid into bloody chaos. The future of Yugoslavia is watched with mounting horror and speculation.

One of the features of a communist dictatorship is that those at the top often have some difficulty explaining away the acquisition of a brand new Rolls-Royce. So it was with the vehicle ordered in early 1953 for the use of President Tito. This Silver Wraith was said to be a gift from Slovenian migrants in Canada, although those who had abandoned Tito's communist rule would, I imagine, be disinclined to purchase such a car. As a matter of interest, when Tito came to buy a new Phantom V in 1960 it was said to be a gift from The Queen. Her Majesty – who has to account for the dis-

Haile Selassie of Ethiopia (left) rides with Marshal Tito in the
latter's 1953 Silver Wraith Mulliner cabriolet (LBLW 37) on a visit
to Kopen, Slovenia in 1959.

ABOVE, AND FOLLOWING PAGES: *President Tito's 1953 Silver Wraith, chassis LBLW 37. The H.J.Mulliner cabriolet (design 7347) was a one-off which included both a division and folding occasional seats.*

posal of her Privy Purse – would, one imagines, be extremely reluctant to dig into her funds to support a man whom most people regarded as a dictator, benevolent or not.

For the first Rolls-Royce the coach-builders H.J. Mulliner were entrusted with the bodywork. This was chassis LBLW 37, which was ordered in mid-March 1953. The design was rather unusual in that its outline appeared to be an extended convertible Bentley of that era. H.J. Mulliner took its inspiration from that drophead and modified it into a four-door with the appropriate radiator. The coachwork design number was 7347. The specification called for speedometer in kilometres, double filament headlamps, a scuttle aerial, a horn muting switch, a high speed fan, automatic gearbox, high frequency horns, extra spare wheel and tyre and also, very unusually, a Phantom IV rear axle with Phantom IV rear brakes, drums and shoes. Two scuttle-mounted lamps were ordered, as well as wing-mounted flag/standard holders. It appears that the hood was made to operate automatically, covering the seven-seater when the weather became inclement. Behind the power division was a pair of forward-facing occasional seats, and nets in the two main rear doors to secure oddments.

The car was ordered through the offices of Boris Snuderl, a well-known Slovenian politician of the mid-fifties, and it was to be delivered to the car maker's agents in Switzerland. From there, the Silver Wraith was moved onwards to Belgrade where the guarantee card was issued in

LEFT, ABOVE: *The Phantom V limousine delivered to Marshal Tito of Yugoslavia in August 1960 was a standard Park Ward limousine with a number of extras such as flag masts to the front wings, extra driving lamps above the bumper and swivelling lamps by the windscreen.*
LEFT, BELOW: *Marshal Tito's 1960 Phantom V limousine outside the offices of Park Ward Ltd in High Road, Willesden just after completion. Flag masts for the front wings and whitewall tyres were among the extras specified.*
ABOVE: *Marshal Tito's Phantom V had a number of alterations made to the facia. Additional instruments were fitted behind the steering wheel, a radio telephone was installed (in the glovebox on the right) and handles at each end of the facia gave control of the scuttle-mounted exterior spotlamps.*

November 1953. After arrival at its destination a radio/telephone was fitted above the right hand rear seat. The cabriolet remained in use, making appearances at most State visits, until President Tito died in 1980. Shortly afterwards, the Rolls-Royce was moved to a Museum in Ljubliana which housed many of the vehicles of the late President. At present, the distance covered by the car has been very moderate.

The second and last Rolls-Royce was a Park Ward-bodied Phantom V, chassis 5 LAT 6. This time the body was a standard Park Ward design,

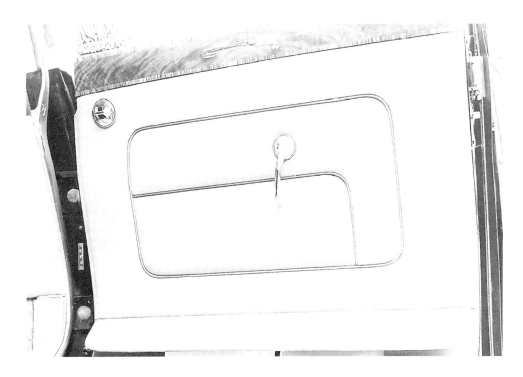

ABOVE: *Door trim on President Tito's Park Ward limousine was in the usual West of England cloth. The switch on the door is for the electrically-operated window.*
BELOW: *The chauffeur's compartment of President Tito's Phantom V, chassis 5LAT 6, was trimmed in the usual leather with folding armrests to both front seats. A sliding picnic table was situated under the facia.*

TOP: *The cloth-trimmed rear seat of Marshal Tito's Phantom V was fitted with a pair of head rests and loose cushions. Silk curtains running on chromium-plated guides were provided to screen both side windows and the rear window.*

ABOVE: *A fitted compartment in the rear armrest of the Tito Phantom V limousine contained gentleman's toilet requisites, including an electric shaver.*

number 980. However, the extra fittings certainly made it something out of the ordinary. It had the by now obligatory scuttle lamps (mostly used, one assumes, for reading roadside signs), two wing flagmasts, a pair of extra-long range lamps fitted just above the bumper, and a set of whitewall tyres. But the interior fitments were not far short of sensational. In the rear compartment, running just behind the electric division, was a full-width sunken shelf, with two fitted picnic tables below it. Two glasses and two mugs were placed in the lockable centre cabinet, whilst two flasks behind could carry hot liquid. Just above floor level was a radio telephone which also had a handset in the front compartment. The windows were power-operated and all the glass area could be covered by blinds, including the rear quarter-lights and backlight. Beige leather in the driver's compartment complemented the light cloth to the rear. With all this in place, the completed Phantom was at last handed over to Auto Serbia and the guarantee became valid from August 1960.

In the boot of President Tito's Phantom V the wheelchanging tools were clipped to the underside of the boot floor with the Dunlop Fort 8.90-15 whitewall-tyred spare wheel housed in the recess beneath. Alongside were the battery and screw jack (on the right) and a tyre pump (on the left).

Tito's Rolls fails to find buyer

A Rolls-Royce that belonged to Tito failed to find a buye when it was put up for sale at 1.4m marks (£530,000), **Reute** **reports from Belgrade.** The 1960 Phantom V, said to have been gift to the then Yugoslav Communist leader from the Queen, ha seating for seven people, and a bar.

The Phantom V limousine purchased by President Tito of Yugoslavia
in 1960. But no sale in 1993, despite the blandishments of the bar
and other special fittings on chassis 5LAT 6.

During its twenty years in service with Tito, the limousine covered a very moderate 20,000 kms (about 12,500 miles). In 1993, the car was finally put up for sale with a reserve of £530,000; not surprisingly this gem of opulence failed to find a buyer and is said to still be in Belgrade. Sadly the present authorities have not sought to continue the Rolls-Royce tradition. Though the awful situation in that benighted country makes it hardly surprising. A symbol of state authority is an empty thing when the state itself has no authority.

AUSTRALASIA

AUSTRALIA

The first Rolls-Royce delivered to the Governor-General was probably in 1922, when chassis 33 KG with an H.J. Mulliner tourer, was handed over to the Head of State. In 1938, W. Shakespeare acquired a Phantom III, chassis 3DL 2 with a Hooper limousine body to design 6443. This was later shipped to Australia in 1941 and used by the Governor-General from 1945 until his return to the United Kingdom in February 1947 when he was appointed as Counsellor of State to King George VI. Three other cars travelled out: WRB 6, (Park Ward limousine), WMB 62 (Thrupp & Maberly limousine) and also a Phantom III, 3AX 195, (with a Barker limousine body). They returned to the UK in early 1947 having had one side-mounted spare wheel added to match the one on the other side of the Phantom III. Chassis 3DL 2 finally left Australia in 1987 when it was sold to a Japanese businessman. It had served honourably until around 1954. Around this time a Park Ward-bodied limousine was acquired for the use of the then Governor-General. This was on Chassis DLW 24, to the design 551, and was eventually handed over to his office in August 1954. The only additions at this time were a clamp over the windscreen for holding a standard and rear compartment curtains. In April 1970 the car was disposed of at auction and has for some time been in the Heytesbury collection in Perth, Western Australia.

Back in the late 1940s a visit to Australia was planned for George VI and Princess Elizabeth. The Federal Government ordered Daimler, then considered to be the Royal car, to produce six magnificent State cars. Sadly the King's illness meant he never undertook the tour but his daughter, the present Queen, used them on her two-month stay in Australia in 1954.

When Her Majesty transferred her allegiance to Rolls-Royce in the late 1950s, the Australian Government followed suit. December 1958 saw the first delivery of what was ultimately, over the next nine years, to amount to four Silver Wraith limousines, two Silver Wraith four-door allweather

ABOVE: *Silver Wraith Park Ward limousine purchased for the use of the Governor-General in 1954. It was sold in 1970.*
BELOW: *Elegant lines of H.J. Mulliner limousine on Silver Wraith Four purchased in 1958; bodies 6174-7 on chassis HLW 45, 46, 48 and 50.*

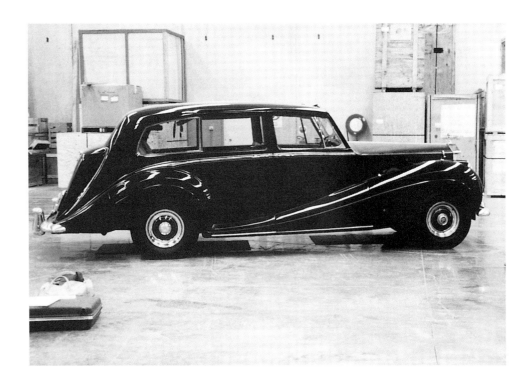

One of the 1958 Silver Wraith H.J. Mulliner limousines. The centre-hinged bonnet was a traditional Rolls-Royce feature but the boot with a drop down lid (left) and mass of dashboard switches were rather dated. Front windows were manually operated.

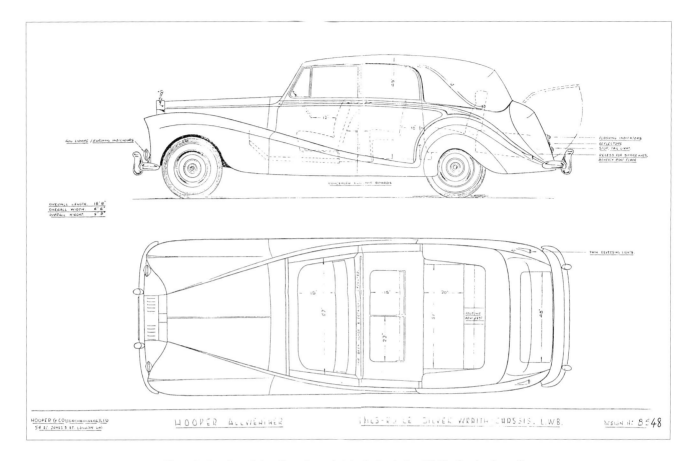

Hooper's drawing of the allweather cabriolet body, design 8548, for the Australian Government. The two Silver Wraith chassis, HLW 47 and HLW 49, were fitted with consecutive bodies (10288, 10289) and delivered in April 1959.

cabriolets, two Silver Cloud long wheelbase four-door cabriolets and two Phantom V limousines. These ten cars were considered necessary because of the vast distances involved in covering Australia and were stationed across the continent.

From first being used for Princess Alexandra of Kent in 1959 until March 1993, the cars were used for all Royal Visits, including nine by The Queen, several by the Queen Mother, Prince and Princess of Wales and many other royal visitors, Presidents and, on one occasion, the Pope. One Silver Wraith limousine (HLW 50) was written off having left the road at speed, leading to the cars being transported between states. However, one of the Silver Cloud III cabriolets (CAL 39) was damaged on a transporter in 1988.

In 1987, the two earliest cabriolets (HLW 47 & 49) were sold off to an Australian museum and the rest were auctioned in April 1994. Why? Well, the official reason is that they were expensive to maintain, used very intermittently and could be unreliable after long storage periods; rubber seals, batteries and fluids became unserviceable. Curiously, three of The Queen's own State cars are older, with much higher mileage than the Australian

BELOW: *The Queen and Duke of Edinburgh riding in one of the Silver Wraith Hooper cabriolets on a visit to Melbourne. Note the handrail for use when standing up.*
OVERLEAF: *The hood is almost flush with the bodywork, affording good visibility.*

cars. The Silver Wraiths, six in all, were specially adapted for the long, dusty roads of Australia and were fitted with oil-bath air cleaners and extra fuel capacity. This last item was a specific request of the Commonwealth of Australia and Rolls-Royce engineers worked to find a position for an extra three gallon tank. Eventually it was fitted alongside the normal eighteen gallon tank and the coachbuilders were notified that this space over the rear axle was not to be utilised. Owners of the Silver Cloud I, a contemporary model of the Silver Wraith, had commented on the need for a larger tank and, from 1959, the extra three gallon tank was offered as an option. Subsequent models had the larger 23 gallon capacity of the Silver Shadow, which arrived in 1965. All six Silver Wraiths were in position for the arrival of HRH The Princess Alexandra of Kent in mid-1959. The H.J. Mulliner seven-seater limousines had been fitted with larger rear quarter lights so the occupant could be more easily glimpsed. Over the rear seats a large transparent section was let into the roof, and as usual the Heraldic Shield and Royal Standard of the Queen as Head of State in Australia could be fitted above the windscreen (HLW 45,46,48 & 50). The four-door Hooper cabriolets, based curiously on a Daimler Royal Stock limousine, were fitted with adjustable individual rear seats, handrails for use when standing and blue

LEFT: *The Queen and Prince Philip have travelled many miles in the Silver Wraith Hooper cabriolets on seven visits to Australia.*
ABOVE: *Prince Charles and Princess Diana also used the 1959 cabriolets.*

front sidelights designed for easy recognition at night. A third cabriolet of the same design was also built for the Emperor of Ethiopia and delivered in 1959. In 1976, John Rowe of Rolls-Royce Motors travelled to Australia to install air-conditioning in all the Silver Wraith cabriolets and H.J. Mulliner limousines.

The cabriolets were so popular that in 1962, the Commonwealth asked Rolls-Royce to supply two more. This time the coachbuilder was Mulliner Park Ward (CAL 37 and 39). The H.J Mulliner design (7484) of a four-door which had been built for an American customer a few years before was located and the coachbuilder set about building the body. Uniquely, the two cars were built with twin headlamps instead of four, as on the current Silver Cloud III introduced in 1962. The four-door Cloud III long wheelbase chassis, like the Hooper cabriolets, was fitted with adjustable seats, handrails and the obligatory extra-range tanks. They entered service in 1963 and when not on VIP visitor duty were housed in Sydney's Birdwood car museum. They do make an appearance every November, however, to convey the Governor-General to the racing's famous social event, the Melbourne Cup. Finally, two standard Phantom Vs (5VF 155 & 5VF 159) were ordered in 1966 towards the end of production of the Phantom V.

One of a pair of special long wheelbase Silver Cloud III cabriolets (chassis CAL 37 and 39) built for the Australian Government in 1963.

ABOVE: *Tyre pump, fitted tray of small tools and emergency winding handles in the Silver Cloud cabriolet's boot.*
OVERLEAF: *One of the pair of Silver Cloud III cabriolets, built to order. Built on a long wheelbase chassis to H.J. Mulliner design 7484 with single headlamps, the cars were finished by Mulliner Park Ward at Willesden.*

Their only apparent distinguishing feature was the blue light over the windscreen with the position for the Heraldic shield behind. More hidden from view was the air-conditioning unit in the boot of the car. As with all the closed cars, extra strong illumination was fitted to the rear compartment so the occupants could be seen at night. The Phantom Vs entered service at the end of 1967.

Today, after three decades of service, the nine remaining cars have

BELOW: *1959 Silver Wraith Hooper cabriolet, fitted with slotted air conditioning outlets and windscreen blinds.*

TOP AND LEFT: *One of the Mulliner Park Ward Phantom V limousines delivered in 1967.*
RIGHT, AND FOLLOWING PAGES:
Catalogue for the Australian Government sale of State cars in 1994.

Collectable Vehicles
from
Australia's History

For Sale
by
Public Tender

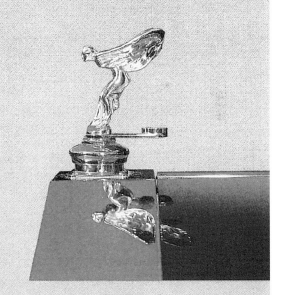

DEPARTMENT OF
ADMINISTRATIVE
SERVICES

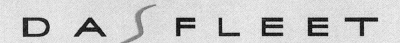

ROLLS-ROYCE

1964 Silver Cloud III Tourers

AUSTRALIA

These outstanding vehicles were purchased from Rolls-Royce in the U.K. and the bodies were hand crafted by the renowned body builders H.J. Mulliner Ltd. Used exclusively for Heads of State at official functions, they are well known for carrying the Governor General to Australia's premier annual racing event, the Melbourne Cup. Both have very low mileage and have been meticulously maintained by the Australian Government.

1958 Silver Wraith LWB Limousines

Outstanding examples of the automotive art. These classic vehicles have been chauffeur driven and scrupulously maintained throughout their colourful 35 year history. They were purchased from Rolls-Royce in the U.K. and hand-built by H.J Mulliner Ltd for the Australian Government. The rarity of these impeccable vehicles is further enhanced as items 4 and 5 have consecutive engine, body and chassis numbers.

1965 Phantom V Limousines

This is a rare opportunity to own a classic vehicle. Impeccably maintained by the Australian Government, they are superb examples of craftsmanship. The bodies were hand-made by H.J. Mulliner Ltd with rich Tan and Cream Cowhide interior trim and dashboards finished in deep Walnut. Their condition is reflected by the fact that they were used exclusively to carry dignitaries and Heads of State at official functions.

Item 2

Colour:	Royal Claret
Interior Trim:	Deer hide - White
Dashboard:	Deep Polished Walnut
Engine:	Rolls-Royce V8 - 6230cc
Transmission:	Four Speed Hydramatic
Engine Number:	P5189
Chassis Number:	CAL 39
Body Number:	S30
Odometer Reading:	11,028 Miles (approx.).

Item 6

Colour:	Royal Claret
Interior Trim:	Deer hide - White
Dashboard:	Deep Polished Walnut
Engine:	Rolls-Royce V8 - 6230cc
Transmission:	Four Speed Hydramatic
Engine Number:	P5315
Chassis Number:	CAL 37
Body Number:	S29
Odometer Reading	20,107 miles (approx.)

Item 4

Colour:	Black
Interior Trim:	Cow hide - Tan (front). Cream (rear)
Dashboard:	Deep Polished Walnut
Engine:	Rolls-Royce 6cyl - 4887cc
Transmission:	Four Speed Hydramatic
Engine Number:	L44H
Chassis Number:	HLW45
Body Number:	6174
Odometer Reading:	74,871 miles (approx.)

Item 5

Colour:	Black
Interior Trim:	Cow hide - Tan (front). Cream (rear)
Dashboard:	Deep Polished Walnut
Engine:	Rolls-Royce 6cyl - 4887cc
Transmission:	Four Speed Hydramatic
Engine Number:	L45H
Chassis Number:	HLW46
Body Number:	6175
Odometer Reading:	61,167 miles (approx.)

Item 7

Colour:	Black
Interior Trim:	Cow hide - Tan (front), Cream (rear)
Dashboard:	Deep Polished Walnut
Engine:	Rolls-Royce 6cyl - 4887cc
Transmission:	Four Speed Hydramatic
Engine Number:	L47H
Chassis Number:	HLW49
Odometer Reading:	55,066 miles (approx.)

Item 1

Colour:	Black
Interior Trim:	Cow hide - Tan (front). Cream (rear)
Dashboard:	Deep Polished Walnut
Engine:	Rolls-Royce V8 - 6230cc
Transmission:	Four Speed Hydramatic
Engine Number:	8S4726
Chassis Number:	5VF159
Odometer Reading:	64,549 miles (approx.)

Item 3

Colour:	Black
Interior Trim:	Cow hide - Tan (front). Cream (rear)
Dashboard:	Deep Polished Walnut
Engine:	Rolls-Royce V8 - 6230cc
Transmission:	Four Speed Hydramatic
Engine Number:	8S4724
Chassis Number:	5VF155
Odometer Reading:	54,757 miles (approx.)

been sold off. Some to wealthy collectors (the four-door cabriolets being particularly desirable), whilst the Silver Wraith limousines will probably end up on hire duties. The auction proved extremely profitable to the present Australian Government.

The two four-door Park Ward Mulliner cabriolets contributed A$850,000 to the revenue alone when they were sold to the United States. One Phantom V fetched over A$100,000 (the other Phantom did not reach its reserve and was sold at auction separately). The three Silver Wraith H.J Mulliner limousines collectively notched up A$220,000; in total the six Rolls-Royces raised close to A$1,200,000. If one considers the two Hooper cabriolets sold in the eighties and the one remaining Phantom to be auctioned, the final figure must be close to A$2,000,000. The written off Silver Wraith limousine which overturned all those years ago, now rebuilt, made a very modest contribution.

Tax free, the ten cars would, overall, have cost around £100,000 between 1959 and 1967 (around A$220,000 today). Certainly, as Sir Henry Royce always claimed, the quality remains long after the cost has been forgotten, and the Australian Ceremonial fleet has given a tenfold return on the initial investment. In retrospect, the Australian Government's decision to go over to Rolls-Royce in 1958 would seem to be a wise one, at the very least in fiscal terms!

At present, Rolls-Royce is unlikely to be excused from official duties on the Continent just yet. The Queen's representative, the Governor-General, has the use of two Phantom VIs which will no doubt be pressed into service until the end of the century, by which time Australia may well have said goodbye to both its monarch and the state Rolls-Royces.

Subsequently, the government of Australia ordered further Phantom VIs PRH 4587, PRH 4731, PRH 4822 and PRH 4839. The latter three were to the PVI S specification with safety features such as front-hinged rear doors. They were for the governments of Queensland, Western Australia and New South Wales respectively and were delivered in January 1973, July 1975 and September 1976.

(As something of an unnecessary but irresistible footnote, we think some of the dates given in the official sales document reproduced on pages 86-87 are wrong: 1963 for the Silver Cloud III tourers, 1967 for the Phantom V limousines.)

NEW ZEALAND

The government of New Zealand was established in September 1907 and given Dominion status at the same time. In 1947 the Statute of Westminster was formally adopted.

In preparation for the King's and Queen's visit to New Zealand in 1949, a number of Daimler cars were purchased and so it was not until 1962 that Phantom Vs came onto the scene. Chassis 5VA 5 and 5VA 15 with standard Mulliner Park Ward limousine bodies were ordered for use on The Queen's 1963 tour. 5VA 15 passed from Government hands some years ago. This was repainted grey over blue and is now resident in the

Phantom V, 5VA 15, a standard Mulliner Park Ward limousine, was ordered by the New Zealand Government for use during The Queen's 1963 tour. It is now in the Southward Motor Museum.

ABOVE: *Phantom V, chassis 5VA15, design 2003. Although originally a single colour, it has since been repainted grey over blue.*
RIGHT: *Frantic activity at Milford Primary School as the Phantom
VI used by Prince Charles and Princess Diana refuses to start during
their visit to New Zealand in 1983. A Daimler came to the rescue.*

Southward Motor Museum alongside the Daimler it replaced. In the late
sixties, two new Phantom VIs were ordered – chassis PRH 4582 and PRH
4583. These were fitted with separate air-conditioning and had the larger
Silver Cloud III engine. PRH 4582 is still in the hands of the New Zealand
authorities, but PRH 4583 was sold off from the Government fleet and has
been used for some time by an Auckland funeral director.

Get out and get under . . . No, the legs sticking out from under this gleaming limousine aren't those of Prince Charles. But it is the royal Rolls Royce, sitting forlornly in the rain at Milford Primary School after it failed to start and left the royal couple temporarily stranded. They were left standing in the rain while red-faced officials peered under the bonnet to find the problem. The breakdown was caused by an ignition failure.

THE AMERICAS

ARGENTINA

In 1946 Juan Domingo Peron became President and his period in office lasted until his overthrow in 1955. He was recalled to occupy the post again in 1973; his widow then occupied the appointment until a coup against her in 1976.

The second Mrs Peron (he was married three times), ordered a specially armour-plated Silver Wraith on chassis WCB 32. This was an H.J.

H.J.Mulliner were noted for their sedanca de ville coachwork on the early post-war Silver Wraith chassis. This example, on 1948 chassis WCB 32, had an armoured rear compartment and was supplied to Eva Peron.

Mulliner sedanca de ville to design 7055 and was delivered in December 1948. This particular vehicle was destined for Buenos Aires as it carried a great deal of armour plating and inch-thick glass. Years later it was sold off and was finally disposed of at a sale in the 1960s when the car collection of John Sword was dispersed.

BRAZIL

The country became an independent empire in 1822 under King Joao VI of Portugal (a cadet line of the ruling Braganza family). In 1889 the King was deposed (Dom Pedro II) and a republic was

Very special Silver Wraith, on chassis LALW 29, delivered to Dr Getulio Vargas, President of Brazil, in 1953. The H.J. Mulliner seven-passenger cabriolet body, number 5438, was to design 7311.

The advent of the longer 133 inch wheelbase Silver Wraith chassis in 1952 afforded coachbuilders considerably more scope, particularly for a vehicle such as this H.J. Mulliner seven-passenger limousine.

proclaimed. The decision by the President of the Republic to order several cars from Rolls-Royce must have come as something of a surprise. The first was a touring limousine on chassis LWSG 53 to the H.J. Mulliner design 7249, followed two months later by another touring limousine (LWSG 74) of a similar design and delivered in January 1953. In December 1952, a lwb version of the Silver Wraith was developed and chassis LALW 27 with an

H.J. Mulliner limousine body was also shipped over in that month. Finally, to complete the quartet, a cabriolet of design 7311 was provided on chassis LALW 29 and was handed over in March 1953.

This latter car merits special attention because it had special chassis-strengthening, a power-operated hood, hand-grips to pillars and rear boot, extra clock and speedometer to rear, oil-bath air cleaner and a two-way radio fitted. White-wall tyres were also specified and the lhd chassis was handed over in April 1953.

This last car is still in service and the incoming President usually goes to his inauguration in the vehicle. It has now completed around 23,000 kilometres, (about 14,000 miles). I regret to say that the whereabouts of the other cars is now no longer known.

CUBA

Cuba's history is one of classic South American political reversals and despotic regimes, punctuated by the formation of a Republican government in 1909 and the arrival of that bête noire of the US, Fidel Castro, who overthrew General Batista in 1959.

In 1926 General Morales took delivery of this left-hand drive 40/50hp
Silver Ghost tourer, chassis S338 RK, manufactured in the Rolls-Royce
of America Inc. factory at Springfield, Massachusetts; the only
Springfield Rolls-Royce ever to be in the service of the state?

Some time before this, in 1926, General Morales ordered an Oxford open tourer on American-built left-hand drive chassis S338 RK. It was delivered in April that year, and the Rolls-Royce Custom Coachwork body was built by Merrimac.

DOMINICAN REPUBLIC

In the middle of the nineteenth century the country now known as the Dominican Republic was founded. President Generalissimo Rafael J. Trujillo was established as dictator after a military coup in 1930 and ruled the country for over thirty years until he was assassinated in 1961.

The General ordered two Phantoms; the first of these was a limousine by Hooper on Phantom III chassis 33 TA delivered in February 1935. The second, ordered for him in 1961, had a body by Park Ward to design 980, built on Phantom chassis 5LBX 30.

However, this limousine was not handed over until after his assassination, arriving in August 1961.

REPUBLIC OF VENEZUELA

The population of the Republic of Venezuela is close to 19 million. In the early part of the last century the Republic gained its independence from Spain. Since 1961 the final executive powers have been held by the President and these are exercised from Caracas.

In 1954, a touring limousine by Hooper to design 8390 on a lhd Silver Wraith chassis, LDLW 60, was sent to Caracas for the possible use of the President. This had an all-metal body finished in super-black with grey leather front and rear plus a grey mohair rug for the interior.

No cabinet was fitted between the seats although for a touring limousine it was unusual in that either of the occasional seats could be used as required. Finally, to add distinction to the car, a set of whitewall tyres was fitted. The vehicle was handed over at the end of November 1954.

ASIA

AFGHANISTAN

The 1964 Constitutional conference ensured that the King of Afghanistan would pass on his title to succeeding generations. However, this was overturned in 1973 and the country has been ruled by a variety of competing agencies ever since. The most obvious to western eyes were the Russians who spent ten years trying to sort out the problems on their border, and failed.

In 1923 HM The King of Afghanistan had in his possession a 20hp Rolls-Royce, chassis 52 S8 with a Barker touring body. This was an early rear-wheel-braked 20hp, which had been delivered that year, just after production of the junior model had begun. In 1925, four-wheel braking became available and this was fitted to 20hp chassis GBM 44, a special Barker-bodied two-door saloon with sliding sunroof, ordered in 1928 after the King had visited the Derby factory.

There was a spate of orders for the Phantom I model from the mid-

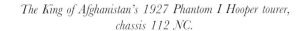

The King of Afghanistan's 1927 Phantom I Hooper tourer,
chassis 112 NC.

twenties onwards. First came a sports body constructed by Barker & Co on chassis 60 YC which was handed over in October 1926. This was followed almost six months later by an open touring body by Hooper & Co on chassis 112 NC. Painted claret and slate blue with claret leather upholstery and Triplex glass fitted throughout, the car was handed over to the local agents in Kabul in the spring of 1927. Barker & Co handled the bulk of orders for the King and indeed built the two remaining Phantom Is. In January 1928 chassis 38 UF was delivered and was a landaulette which utilised the Beatonson system for the folding head. In the following summer the final Phantom I, a cabriolet on chassis 3 AL, was handed over.

The final chassis allocated by Derby was the mighty V-12 engined Phantom III on chassis 3DL 200. This was a Park Ward-bodied two-door with an all-over aluminium finish. The car was a true convertible and was fitted with a side-mounted spare wheel. The body number was 4633 and the Park Ward coachwork, which included King Zahir Shah's crest on the

Park Ward described this very unusual body, on Phantom III chassis 3DL 200, as a two/four-seater coupé cabriolet. Abandoned and decaying in Kabul, it has bullet holes in the body but is probably restorable.

Abandoned in the Kabul Palace gardens, the King of Afghanistan's
Phantom III, 3DL 200, is missing some parts and the facia is splintering.

doors, cost £923. The completed car was handed over in December 1939, by which time Rolls-Royce was – of course – busy transferring its attention elsewhere. Only recently this car was discovered abandoned in the Kabul Palace gardens.

The monarch, now in his eighties, has lived in Rome for most of his life and is unlikely to return to Kabul.

BAHRAIN

Bahrain has been a constitutional monarchy since 1971, and prior to this was ruled by an Arabian prince. The population is roughly half a million.

The Khalifa family has exercised power over many centuries. In recent years the ruling family has purchased a considerable number of cars from Crewe. Probably the first of these was the Silver Wraith chassis, which was available only with a coachbuilt body.

The first car delivered was on chassis ALW 28 and was to design 7276. This was the first such sketch specifically drawn for the 6 inch longer 133-inch wheelbase. Oil had been discovered in the early 1930s and by the

ABOVE: *Peter Wharton of Park Ward prepared this wash drawing of the Ruler of Bahrain's Phantom V landaulette, design 2047, on chassis 5VD 33.*

BELOW: *The Ruler of Bahrain's long wheelbase Silver Shadow was distinguished by special stainless steel trim to the sills and flared wheelarches.*

ABOVE: *Screen pillar-mounted lamps, a shield and extended stainless steel trim curving down to the bumper on the Ruler of Bahrain's Silver Shadow lwb delivered in the mid-1970s.*
RIGHT: *The interior was to FSS specification with padding and recessed switches. Rev counter and woodrim steering wheel were special features.*

beginning of the 1950s around 42,000 barrels were gushing from the oil wells every day. The lwb Silver Wraith had been ordered in the spring of 1952 and was delivered in September. It is very likely that this H.J. Mulliner limousine remained in service until the advent of a Mulliner Park Ward drophead coupé on Silver Cloud III chassis SGT 593C (design 2045) delivered in August 1964.

Just a dozen years after the introduction of the H.J. Mulliner Silver

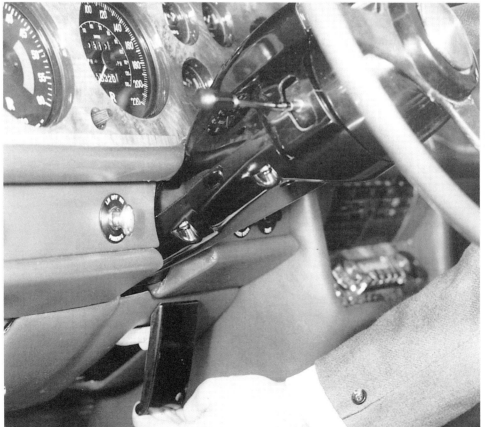

Wraith, the authorities in Bahrain ordered a State landaulette to design 2047. This was, in reality, similar to the President of Tunisia's but based on the four headlamp design introduced almost two years before and was on chassis 5LVD 33. It was equipped with scuttle-mounted long-range lamps, flagstaff to mascot and roof, an illuminated shield to front and rear; rear view aspect was to some extent reduced because of the narrowness of the rear aperture through the manually-operated spring-assisted black leather landaulette portion.

At the 1965 Earls Court Motor Show Rolls-Royce exhibited a new Mulliner Park Ward ceremonial State Landaulette (design 2052) on which the whole of the roof from the division rearwards could be opened. This Phantom V on the Rolls-Royce stand was chassis 5VD 83, the second ceremonial car built, and unusually had the rear compartment trimmed in tan hide (instead of cloth). It was purchased by the Ruler of Bahrain and delivered in March 1966.

The duo were joined in the early seventies by a Silver Shadow lwb, again with scuttle-mounted long range lamps, front and rear shields and a mascot-mounted flagstaff. By now, of course, full air-conditioning was standard and the car was supplied lhd.

In 1972 the new Phantom VI became the basis for a splendid H.J. Mulliner, Park Ward limousine, this time to the fss specification with front-hinged doors. This was on chassis PRX 4720.

As far as is known, all the cars purchased have remained in the possession of the Ruling Family of Bahrain.

BRUNEI

It is often convenient journalese to describe the Sultanate of Brunei as 'oil-rich'. This is actually a simplification, as Brunei exports not only oil but natural gas, especially to the Pacific rim. The Sultan has been described as probably the richest man in the world, and acceded to his title in 1967 as His Majesty Sultan Haji Hassanal Bolkiah Mu'izzaddin Waddaulah. In just over a quarter of a century, His Majesty has acquired just about every model of Rolls-Royce known to man.

ABOVE: *Stainless steel trim to the sills and wheelarches, chromium-plated door centre pillars and a roof-mounted standard are some of the extras on this Phantom VI owned by the Sultan of Brunei.*
FOLLOWING PAGES: *The Sultan of Brunei's first Phantom VI, on chassis PRH 4642, one of his earliest, if not the first, Rolls-Royce acquisition, was delivered in September 1971 and has rear-hinged back doors.*

It is most likely that one of the first of these was a Phantom VI on chassis PRH 4642, which was probably given to his father after the arrival of a second Phantom VI in the PGH series. This was followed in the early eighties by a Silver Spur stretched limousine with six doors, an identification light on the roof and a flagstaff just behind. The Sultan was reputed to have ordered two (one for his wife) and the cost, with all the appointments, was said to be around £140,000 each. Robert Jankel of Weybridge, under contract to Rolls-Royce Motors, extended two standard Silver Spurs and gave them six seats, a colour TV and video recorder, plus a two-way communi-

The Sultan of Brunei's stretched Silver Spur limousine, built by Robert Jankel under contract to Rolls-Royce. The extra pair of rear doors were added after the bodyshell had been cut and extended by 36 inches.

cation system (thus avoiding lowering the division bullet-proof glass to the chauffeur's compartment). At that time they were the longest Rolls-Royce limousines available at 20ft 6in in length. This is hardly surprising since 36ins were added to the wheelbase.

At the 1974 Earls Court Motor Show a ceremonial State Landaulette, to Mulliner Park Ward design 2052, was exhibited on the Rolls-Royce stand. It was on chassis PRH 4793 and was later sold to the Sultan and delivered in 1975.

Probably the greatest prize of any collector was the acquisition of the last Phantom VI to be made. This was on LWH 10426 and based rather loosely on the 2047 design, meaning that the folding leather head was lowered from the rear standing pillar. I recall seeing this fine State Landaulette in the showrooms in Maidenhead where it was on public view. Amongst its elegant features was a clock mounted into the division, with a matching altimeter on the other side.

When I talked to Roger Cra'ster he told me that, while working for Rolls-Royce, he had acquired for the Sultan many of his Rolls-Royce and Bentley cars; more than likely around 130 vehicles!

HONG KONG

In 1997, the Crown Colony of Hong Kong will revert to Chinese authority. The present Governor, Chris Patten, is unlikely to continue to serve in that post after June 1997. Meanwhile, Governor Patten is negotiating over the future of nearly six million inhabitants.

The Phantom V landaulette to the Park Ward design 1000 was prepared over three decades ago and, in the case of Hong Kong, will probably survive the millennium under different ownership. The design 1000 is in the same style as the car prepared for HM Queen Elizabeth, The Queen

Prince Charles rides in the Governor of Hong Kong's Phantom V Park Ward landaulette on a visit to the colony. An advantage of this type of body is that when the top is closed it becomes a limousine.

ABOVE AND RIGHT: *The Governor of Hong Kong's Phantom V,*
chassis 5BV 7, dates from 1961. It carries no number plates but has
gilded crowns instead. The leather-covered landaulette roof is
manually operated.

Mother, whose car was given the design 1104. The differences between
1104, 1000 and the President of Tunisia's vehicle are marginal. The Queen
Mother's car has a glass section set into the roof over the rear compartment,
which is one distinguishing trait. Another is the number plate plinth on the
boot lid. Both have a roof-mounted police light, with shield-holder just
behind. Perhaps only the eagle-eyed would notice that the boot-lid handle
on the Queen Mother's Phantom V is of the vertical variety.

Governor Patten's limousine was shipped to Hong Kong in February
1961 on chassis 5BV 7 and has now served six governors. Since making its

first appearance at Government House in late April 1961, the vehicle has covered around 100,000 miles. Regular servicing is carried out in the Crown Colony about every six weeks or so, with major overhauls taking place every ten years. The Governor's landaulette carries no number plates, having only a gilt crown at the front and rear. It possesses tiny lights positioned on the wings, just in front of the rear view mirrors, which shine on to the appropriate flag flown from just behind the mascot. Some years ago a pair of arm-slings were installed just by the rear standing pillars.

INDIA

For almost seventy years, India was defined by many as the jewel in the imperial crown. No standing army could control a population close to 700 million. State ceremonial played its part.

In 1909, the Earl of Minto took delivery of a Barker-bodied Silver Ghost (chassis 1113) which was used both by himself and, from 1911, the Viceroy Lord Harding. This landaulette was replaced by another Silver Ghost, again with a Barker body. A curious interregnum followed, with the Willingdons taking a Daimler limousine with centre seats which was copied by Lord Linlithgow (who was to be replaced in mid-1943 by Lord Wavell). However, as soon as Linlithgow took up his appointment in 1936, he ordered a Hooper-built body for his Phantom III chassis 3AZ 47, ordered in 1935, which again sported the centre seats so beloved of George V. The limousine (design 6419) was finished in dark blue with additional covers fitted over the blue seats.

Above the fully-opening windscreen was a blue roof light with an attachment behind on which to fly a standard. Full-length louvres ran along the bonnet and figured walnut woodwork was included, as was a Viscount's coronet on the main doors. As with His Majesty's Daimler cars, the roof was raised by almost 6in throughout its length. The vehicle served all three Viceroys and was retired in 1947, when a new Silver Wraith was ordered.

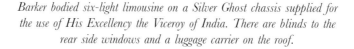

Barker bodied six-light limousine on a Silver Ghost chassis supplied for the use of His Excellency the Viceroy of India. There are blinds to the rear side windows and a luggage carrier on the roof.

Special Hooper limousine on Phantom III chassis 3AZ 47 delivered to Lord Linlithgow in 1936. The roof was raised by six inches to accommodate the Viceroy's cocked hat. The louvred bonnet was to aid cooling.

This was on Chassis WVA 6 and was a rather uninspiring Park Ward limousine which was shipped to India very close to the time that the country achieved independence. The car, which was to design 17, was handed over in August 1947 when it was used by Earl Mountbatten, who had offered to remain in office as the new Governor-General. Jinnah was to appoint himself to the post however, and Earl Mountbatten eventually left in June 1948.

And so the power of the Viceroys and their fabulous cars faded from history and only the grandeur of the Phantom III remains. It is now in the collection of a Bombay businessman, who probably appreciates that the limousine was given an additional odd number in the chassis numbering system which makes the elderly vehicle even more distinctive.

IRAN

The story of the Shahs of Iran is one of deposition, re-establishment and, finally, abolition. In 1925, Prime Minister Reza Khan abolished the Qajar Dynasty and established himself in December that year as the legitimate heir. In 1941, he resigned in favour of the Crown Prince who thus became Mohammed Reza Shah Pahlavi. In 1979, the Shah departed under popular pressure, and Ayatollah Khomeini became

BELOW: *Phantom I Hooper limousine, on chassis 72 DC, delivered to the Shah of Persia in 1926. The interior was lavishly appointed. Note the louvres on the bonnet to aid cooling in the Tehran heat.*
BOTTOM: *Unidentified landaulette – probably also by Hooper on a Phantom I chassis.*

ABOVE, AND FOLLOWING PAGES: *The Shah of Iran's 1922 40/50hp Silver Ghost Hooper cabriolet, chassis 38 PG, photographed at Crewe in the 1980s after refurbishment. Note the tiny rear window.*

the leader. In 1922, Sultan Ahmed Shah ordered a 40/50hp Silver Ghost which at that time had only two-wheel brakes. Chassis 38 PG was allocated and on it Hooper and Co built a cabriolet body. The car was delivered in late June 1923. In the late seventies, this fine enclosed cabriolet was returned to Crewe for attention, at the same time as a rare Phantom IV.

In early 1926, the new Shah decided to order a Phantom I with a Hooper body on chassis 72 DC. This fine vehicle had plush interior upholstery and gold fittings. There were two extra seats which could be made to fold flush behind the division as required. Because of the daytime heat in Tehran, the bonnet was fitted with louvres along its length. As usual, side-mounted spare tyres were fitted. The car was handed over in July 1926, with crests added to the doors.

The next chassis ordered was a Phantom III 3DL 138, which was bodied as a touring limousine by Park Ward and delivered in the spring of 1939. This chassis had the important engine modifications including four-part cylinder heads, single valve springs and solid tappets. The car was painted black with a grey velvet interior. Coachwork features included a streamlined swept-back seating four, a sunroof at the front, French-polished walnut and no built-in number plates. The design was 4619 and the car was off test on 5 January and handed over on 22 April 1939.

The Shah of Iran's 1956 Phantom IV limousine, chassis 4CS 6, and 1922 Silver Ghost cabriolet, chassis 38 PG, outside the service department at Crewe in the 1980s. Both cars are now back in Tehran.

The Phantom IV had the largest radiator of any post-war Rolls-Royce and it was much taller than the Silver Ghost's (behind). The louvres (here shut) were operated by thermostatic control. Lucas R100 lamps contributed to the impressive appearance.

In mid-1950, the Shah decided to purchase a Phantom IV which was fitted with a power-operated hood, headlamps at the extremity of the wings, whitewall tyres and purdah glass all round. The rear wheels were fully enclosed and the car also possessed twin scuttle-mounted long range lamps and electric windows throughout. The car was totally unsatisfactory in use, and after a sojourn in Rome with an unsuitable driver (recruited from the embassy), chassis 4AF 6 (design 7205) was eventually dismantled and scrapped at the Hythe Road in June 1959 because of scuttle-shake. The body was sold off for use on a Phantom III by Simmons of Mayfair, who then disposed of it in the U.S.A.

The only other Phantom IV purchased by the Shah of Iran was to Hooper's design 8425 on the last chassis to be allocated by Crewe 4CS 6. Like all the chassis in the final run, a B81 engine and automatic

119

ABOVE AND BELOW: *The Shah of Iran's Phantom IV had an armoured rear compartment with bullet-proof glass. The glass roof panel could be covered by a sliding steel panel inside. The sloping boot offered little luggage space.*

ABOVE AND BELOW: *The coachwork of the Shah of Iran's Phantom IV, 4CS6,*
to design 8425 was almost identical to King Faisal's car (4BP 1). Rear wheel
spats and chromium-plated trim to wings and sills were a Hooper feature.

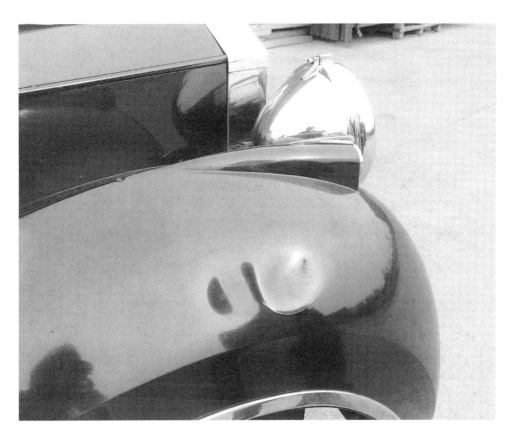

The Shah of Iran's Phantom IV had been returned to Rolls-Royce Motors'
Crewe service department for attention to both mechanicals and the bodywork.
This work was never undertaken and the car was returned to Tehran with this
dent still in evidence.

transmission were offered with a column-mounted gear selector. Like all Phantom IVs these were 8.00-17in tyres on special wheels with ten securing studs and bolt-on balance weights. This was a touring limousine supplied with bullet-proof glass to the rear, including the rear quarterlights, electric windows and a splinter-proof glass section set into the roof. Interior trim was in grey leather; exposed R100 headlamps and a medium, short and long wave radio was fitted. The interior woodwork was lightly bleached, walnut flame veneer and the car was finished all over in deep maroon. As a matter of interest, the cost of a Phantom IV chassis on this last series reached £3,950, plus £4,200 for the bodywork. Geoffrey Francis applied his heraldic decoration to the rear doors and the car was sent up to Crewe in November 1956 for testing. The car was eventually delivered in late 1956 but not before someone had reported a small nick in the limousine's windshield, although it was established that the bullet-proofing would not be affected in any way by the attention of the glass polisher. Twenty years later, the car was still impounded at Crewe awaiting the payment of cash until, at last, two clients – the Ayatollah and the eldest son of the late Shah – were willing to pay. By this time, the touring limousine had covered just over 32,000 km in almost 40 years. The Silver Ghost and the Phantom IV were last reported to be in a Tehran museum.

The Shah was very quick off the mark to order a Phantom V with a Park Ward body. This was on Chassis 5LAS 39 and was delivered to Iran in June 1960. Six years later, the Shah was keen to acquire another Phantom V, this time on 5 LVF 29, a ceremonial State Landaulette which was handed over in August 1966.

The fifth chassis of the new Phantom, announcd in 1968, was destined for Iran and the Shah took delivery in 1969. Chassis PRX 4182 had a number of modifications – including uprated springs, stronger 16in wheels and 10-stud hubs – to cope with a fully-armoured body. The complete car weighed about 8,500 lb. After taking delivery of his first Camargue in 1975, the Shah ordered another two Phantom VI limousines, but neither was armour-plated. They were PRX 4860 and PRX 4861, both lhd and fitted with television, and delivered in 1977. When the cars were ordered the Shah was quoted £23,800 per car but inflation took this to £43,405 by the time of delivery. The Shah protested about the increased cost and so Rolls-Royce Motors charged him £34,275 for each car, making a loss on the sale. Sadly, both cars received minimal usage and one was reported to be up for sale recently with just a delivery mileage on the odometer.

The Shah also had a variety of Silver Cloud III convertibles, a few Corniches and at least two Camargues.

IRAQ

Turkey renounced sovereignty over Iraq in 1921, when the Emir Faisal was elected King. Until his assassination in July 1958, the monarchy held sway over the country.

The Prince Regent of Iraq purchased this Phantom III, chassis 3CM 197, secondhand in 1944. It had been built in 1938 for Hooper's managing director and this sedanca de ville, design 7315, appeared to have been a one-off. The imposing frontal appearance (right) may have attracted the Prince Regent; it had the tallest radiator of any Rolls-Royce, flanked by P100 headlamps.

In 1928, His Majesty of the Hashemite Kingdom of Iraq placed an order for an open touring vehicle on the Phantom I chassis with a body by Fountains & Company. This coachbuilding establishment was resident at the time in Enfield, Middlesex and was one of a number of companies resident on the outskirts of London which specialised in constructing bodies to order. The Phantom I (chassi 88 UF) was delivered in June 1928.

King Faisal The First was replaced in the early forties by the Prince Regent, until the accession of King Faisal II in 1953. Just after taking up his regency, the new Head of State bought a number of Phantom IIIs. In 1944, he purchased a Hooper sedanca de ville on Chassis 3CM 197. Originally this had been used as a 'stock' vehicle for the Managing Director of Hooper & Co, G. Sclater-Booth, until he sold the vehicle that year. It was sent out to Baghdad and did not return until 1953. This was to design 7315 and painted black and brown with typical Hooper touches to the rear

compartment which had a concealed front opening roof panel over the driver. The chassis was passed off test in March 1938 and in almost nine years in Iraq covered about 30,000 miles. Today the car is kept at a museum in Fort Worth, Texas and has run up only another 30,000 miles.

In 1937, The Clyde Auto Co ordered a limousine for D.C. Bowser of Argaty near Doune, Scotland and chassis 3CM 145 was delivered in April 1938. In 1945 this limousine, to design 7186, was delivered to HRH The Prince Regent and was a full six/seven-seater. Although records do not recall the situation, it seems that when the Phantom IVs arrived the car may well have returned to the United Kingdom in the mid-fifties, especially as the Prince Regent lost his status as Head of State.

In April 1937, Phantom III chassis 3BU 132 was delivered to Baron Glanely, who kept the car until 1942. The Hooper limousine was then handed over to the Royal Aircraft Establishment and some four years later came under the ownership of the Prince Regent, who kept it until it was returned to the United Kingdom in 1954. The car was painted black (over yellow), had a centre division and twin side mounts. The interior was completed in West of England cloth to the rear, and leather to the front seats. The design number allocated to the car was 6744.

*Perhaps it was the striking original yellow and grey colour scheme of
this lwb Silver Wraith, on chassis LALW 31, with Franay sedanca de
ville coachwork that prompted the Crown Prince of Iraq to purchase it
from the 1952 Paris Motor Show.*

The final Phantom III acquired by the Prince Regent was chassis 3 AZ
202, with a body by Gurney Nutting, in 1949. It had started life with Lord
George Gee, and moved on two years later to the Railways Board before
ending up in Iraq. This was a sedanca de ville with a rather raked windscreen and B posts, and was again fitted with twin side mounts. It could seat
five people in the rear with two up front.

With regard to the Phantom IVs, Chassis 4BP 1 and 4BP 3 proceeded
through the Hooper works almost together. By this time King Faisal of Iraq
had ascended the throne and the Prince Regent was, to some extent, in the
shadows. The King chose design 8361, a seven-seater limousine, which was
fitted with an oil-bath air cleaner, colonial front springing, and speedometer in km. The car was finished in black all over with a red picking out line,
with red leather in the interior and a mohair rug to match the red carpet.
Built-in number plates were also required, with a pennant holder to hold a

suitable flag and affix a suitable grant of arms to the rear doors. A centre cabinet, holding a receiver (Model 4300) was also supplied. The roof over the rear compartment could be covered at will by a shutter and electric windows were installed all round. A folding rear armrest with silver-backed clothes-brushes and a hinged mirror with space for small articles was also provided. There were also two folding polished tables on the back of the division. The completed car was handed over on the 26 March 1953 where it left almost at once for France.

Meanwhile, the other car, 4BP 3, which almost matched (but had a more angular roof to the rear, on design 8370, and was really a touring limousine) was also nearing completion. This time, the glass section to the rear roof was omitted. However, the Prince Regent did request a rear seat squab adjuster which would enable him to relax out of view. As the car was not completed as a limousine, only one sideways seat was fitted to the offside. For security, the rear compartment armrest was fitted with a secret recess which came with a Yale lock. Again, electric windows were fitted and the

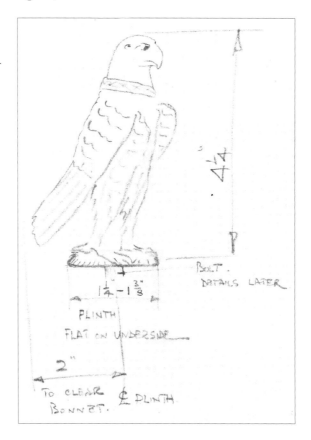

Sketch giving the salient dimensions for the special mascot required by King Faisal II of Iraq. The Eagle of Hatra was fitted to the radiator cap of his Silver Cloud, chassis LSGE 252, with drophead coupé body by Hooper & Co. The car was for the King's private use.

car was ready for shipment to France on the 26 March 1953. Some years later this car (4BP 3) was acquired by the King of Jordan and has been the subject of a total rebuild at P & A Wood. Curiously, the car left Iraq because it was returned to the UK for the fitment of refrigeration in 1958 The Phantom IV had been part of the collection of Sam Ornstein in New Jersey until 1987.

In 1952, the Crown Prince acquired a lwb Silver Wraith with, chassis number LALW 31, in France. Franay had provided the coachwork, which was fitted with gold-plated companions in the rear arm rests, two storage compartments (possibly for guns in the front wings) and the interior was trimmed with leather in the front and cloth in the rear. The bodywork was a sedanca de ville. In late 1952 the then Crown Prince purchased this car off the Paris Show stand where it had the distinction of being the most expensive car (£8,000) and later King Faisal II (as he became) used the car on a State Visit to France. Many years later the car turned up in the United Kingdom, where for many years it has been in the ownership of a lady in Boston Spa, Yorkshire.

In late 1957, His Majesty decided that he would order, for his private use, a drophead coupé on a Silver Cloud (chassis LSGE 252). The lhd vehicle was to Hooper design 8530 and had a host of extra modifications for the King's personal use. The car had a special compartment on the rhd side with an illuminated drawer which contained solid silver Asprey toilet requisites for his adored wife. The car had an automatic hood which, when lowered, was concealed behind a metal cover. Two veneered cabinets to the rear of the main seats held picnic equipment and there was also a refrigerated cabinet for holding liquid refreshment – the very first of its kind – which cost some £360. The mascot on the radiator cap was an 'Eagle of Hatra'; with two flame-thrower spot lamps and with a louder than normal horn, the car could be driven through traffic with zest. The completed coupé was finished in Mercedes-Benz blue with the veneered woodwork in ice-birch with a zebrano inlay. Finally a pair of watches was supplied by the London company Negretti and Zambra.

(Chassis LSGE 252, sold to an Arabian Prince, was sold to an American collector in the late seventies, having completed a mere 6,000 km. One of the minor casualties of the Gulf conflict was the disappearance of seventy-seven Rolls-Royces and Bentleys from Kuwait.)

ABOVE: *Queen Margrethe II of Denmark leaves the royal palace in Copenhagen in the 1958 Silver Wraith Hooper limousine, chassis LGLW 25, originally built for King Frederik IX.*

RIGHT: *In Britain a shield with a crown is never used on the car conveying the sovereign but is displayed on following suite cars carrying household officials, on a car conveying the sovereign's representative or on cars used by other members of the Royal Family. All official Royal cars in the United Kingdom carry a blue police identification lamp above the windscreen.*

TOP LEFT: *The last Rolls-Royce Phantom VI, a landaulette on chassis LWH 10426, completed on 17 December 1991. Registered 1200 TU, it was built for Rolls-Royce Motor Cars but later sold to the Sultan of Brunei.*
BOTTOM LEFT: *This 1938 Phantom III (3CP 116) began life as a Windovers cabriolet in India. In the fifties, Hooper modified it for Portugal.*
ABOVE AND OVERLEAF: *The 1958 Park Ward landaulette, on Silver Wraith chassis LGLW 24, supplied to Queen Juliana of the Netherlands.*

The people of Slovenia are said to have 'presented' this unusual H.J. Mulliner seven-passenger cabriolet on a Silver Wraith chassis (LBLW 37) to Marshal Tito of Yugoslavia in 1953.

*Marshal Tito's four-door cabriolet was a one-off H.J. Mulliner body to
design 7347. The unusual high boot line resulted from the power-
operated hood and the need to accommodate its mechanism.*

*The 1948 Silver Wraith H.J. Mulliner limousine on chassis WCB 17 (left)
was the first of four Rolls-Royces ordered by General Franco. The three H.J.
Mulliner-bodied Phantom IVs, a four-door cabriolet (4AF 18) and two limousines
(4AF 14 and 4AF 16), are still used by the Spanish royal family.*

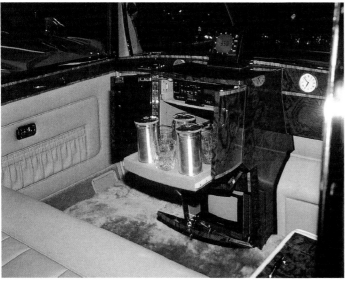

ABOVE AND LEFT: *1986 Phantom VI Mulliner Park Ward State Landaulette on chassis GWH 10153 for the Sultan of Selangor. It was then the most expensive Rolls-Royce ever delivered, with a host of special fittings such as solid 24 carat gold crests on the doors. Inside the cocktail cabinet, surmounted by an electronic ship's compass, were a video recorder and pull-out drinks tray with silver insulated flasks and crystal glasses. The television is visible below.*

RIGHT: *One of a pair of 1959 Silver Wraith Hooper cabriolets, owned by the Australian Government, used to convey Her Majesty Queen Elizabeth II on several state visits down under.*

In May 1967 the Amir of Kuwait took delivery of this Mulliner Park Ward limousine on Phantom V chassis 5LVF 123. It was supplied with the optional refrigeration system (air conditioning) mounted in the boot.

RIGHT: *Some customers had special provision made to mount their own mascots in place of the Rolls-Royce Spirit of Ecstasy. The King of Thailand's ornate glass mascot depicted a Garuda and is shown surmounting the radiator of his armoured Phantom VI limousine (chassis PGH 115) delivered in 1980. The car's ivory-coloured paintwork helped to reflect the heat.*

BELOW RIGHT: *Before the granting of independence in 1947, India's ruling princes were among Rolls-Royce's best customers. Some continued to buy cars afterwards. Typical was the Maharajah of Mysore who took delivery of an unusual Hooper touring saloon on Silver Wraith chassis WGC 31 in 1949. The car illustrated is not actually that ordered by the Maharajah, but belongs to Terence Morley and is one of only seven examples with this body. The rear-hinged front doors and rear wheel spats were pre-war features retained in design 8181. The first appearing on the Hooper stand at the 1948 Earls Court Motor Show.*

ABOVE: *This Park Ward landaulette, on Silver Wraith chassis FLW 75, was delivered to the Governor of Nyasaland (now Malawi) in 1958. Landaulette bodies were particularly favoured by colonial governors as the open aspect easily accommodated the large hats worn on formal occasions.*

LEFT: *1975 Silver Shadow long wheelbase (LRX 22245) originally owned by Emperor Bokassa of the Central African Republic and now in Switzerland. Mulliner Park Ward spliced the extra 4 inches into the floor and roof of the standard Shadow bodyshell and lengthened the rear doors. Build, trimming and painting were then completed at Crewe.*

ABOVE: *1958 Silver Wraith Hooper landaulette on chassis HLW 35, supplied
to the Governor of West Nigeria, still retains its original colour scheme.*
BELOW: *South African 1937 Phantom III Hooper landaulette now in Germany.*

JAPAN

Japan has been a monarchy since 1899, hereditary in the male line only. The first purchase of Rolls-Royce cars was in 1920, when the Imperial Household ordered two Silver Ghosts for the Emperor Taisho.

These were on chassis 21 UE and 38 UE. The design for the pair was 656 and both were finished as limousines.

The cars were painted imperial red with black mouldings and fine-lined in gold. They were equipped with an exhaust car heater and all accessories were finished in brass. Both were shipped on board the *S.S. Inaba Maru* on

It 1920 Japan's Imperial Household purchased its first Rolls-Royce.
This 40/50hp Silver Ghost tourer is probably the car used by the
Regent in Taipei, Formosa.

Open tourer coachwork was especially suited to use in Far Eastern countries such as Japan. This 40/50hp Silver Ghost, with only two-wheel brakes, is probably chassis 58 YG used by the Japanese Regent in Formosa.

8 July. In 1933 or 1934, the Silver Ghosts were dismantled and the engines were used to power an emergency water supply to the Palace! An ignomious fate for such examples of engineering and craftsmanship.

There is a query over the supply of an open tourer with Hooper coachwork on chassis 58 YG which was used by the Regent in Taipei, Formosa. This chassis did not leave Derby until mid-September 1922. It still exists today, but with a locally-built Packard limousine body.

Evocative pageantry of an age long gone. This 40/50hp Silver Ghost, probably conveying the Japanese Regent of Formosa, carries a special mascot and is accompanied by a Vauxhall.

Because of League of Nations sanctions in the mid-1930s, Rolls-Royce were prevented from supplying up-to-date cars. In their absence, Mercedes-Benz stepped in to provide quite a few Imperial limousines. Following the Second World War, an enquiry was received to supply a Silver Wraith chassis. This was numbered FLW 90 and was rhd. There were a number of features on this car which set it apart from run of the mill limousines: a much smaller back light, full air-conditioning, a secondary battery, hooks for

131

In 1921 Emperor Taisho of Japan took delivery of two 40/50hp Silver Ghosts, chassis 21 UE and 38 UE, with identical Hooper limousine bodies.

transporting the car by rail and an adjustable front driving seat. The vehicle had blinds to the rear quarter-lights, an eight-day clock, double glazed quarter-light windows, and adjustable rear seating. An oil-bath air cleaner was also provided. Finally the complete limousine was painted black all over with blue leather upholstery in front and an ivory-tinged cloth in the rear. The car was sent for testing and the guarantee became effective on 27 September 1957. However, Rolls-Royce's (or rather Hooper's) troubles were

ABOVE, AND LEFT: *1957 Silver Wraith Hooper limousine, body no. 10239 on chassis FLW 90, to design 8460 delivered to the Emperor of Japan and pictured outside the Imperial Castle in Tokyo. Note the small oval rear window and shield in front of the radiator.*
FOLLOWING PAGES: *Phantom V Park Ward eight-passenger limousine, chassis 5 BV 91, supplied to the Japanese Imperial Household in 1961. It was requested to have eight inches of ground clearance.*

not over. The Imperial Household Agency complained that the rear seat was not low enough, the air-conditioning was not up to standard and that the promised radio set had not materialised. However, the Japanese Emperor eventually adjusted to his car, and was undeterred from ordering a new Phantom some three years later.

This was to design 980, a full eight-passenger limousine on chassis 5BV 91 which, again, was fitted with full refrigeration, chassis-hooks for rail transportation and an additional battery in the boot. The complete

135

The new Emperor of Japan elected to ride in his Corniche convertible after his enthronement ceremony in November 1990. Note the special wing mirrors and rising sun symbol cast on the door.

Phantom was handed over in March 1961. A second Phantom V, chassis 5VA 29, was ordered in late 1962, which incorporated all the design improvements for the Sanction II cars. The completed H.J. Mulliner, Park Ward design 2003 was handed over in January 1963. Finally, a Phantom VI (PRH 4732) was delivered to the Imperial Household in 1974 (though the records state that it was shipped to 'Mr T Miki' in Osaka, so we cannot be sure that this was an Imperial car). There was an important difference; it was armour-plated and had a body by H.J. Mulliner, Park Ward.

However, in 1965, Prince Motors (later acquired by Nissan) stepped in to provide State transport and from that time have had the special responsibility of conveying the monarch around Japan. Contrary to popular belief, they were also entrusted with transporting the body of Emperor Hirohito in 1989. More recently, in the autumn of 1990, a splendid Rolls-Royce Corniche II on chassis MCH 30350, with replaceable rear seats, special rear-view mirrors, and rising suns cast on the doors was made available for the new Emperor, enthroned in that year.

JORDAN

The present Kingdom of Jordan was established in the late forties from the rule of the Amir Abdullah, who became King of the Hashemite Kingdom of Jordan until his assassination in 1951. His first son then assumed the mantle until he was succeeded in 1952 by King Hussein, currently Head of State.

At the time of the Suez War it was, not surprisingly, thought best to avoid buying British and it was not until 1960 that His Majesty ordered a Park Ward-bodied Phantom V to the design 980. This was on chassis 5LBV 5 and delivered in December that year. In August 1967, The Queen Mother took delivery of a standard-bodied H.J. Mulliner, Park Ward design 2003 on chassis 5LVF 139, but it seems likely that His Majesty decided to adopt the car for himself after her death.

One of the greatest curiosities was King Hussein's decision to purchase and restore the Phantom IV originally built for the Prince Regent of Iraq. This was on chassis 4BP 3 and was a Hooper touring limousine to design 8370. At present, the vehicle still resides in the workshops of the Essex Roll-Royce distributors P & A Wood.

KUWAIT

The State of Kuwait has been independent for some years and has had a long-running conflict with its neighbour Iraq, culminating in the war of 1991.

The Al-sabah family has exercised considerable authority over the Kuwaiti emirate, and in the early fifties ordered three Phantom IVs which considering the size of the country (only 6,880 square miles) was certainly a belt and braces approach. The state is of course very wealthy, and, as has been mentioned earlier, nearly eighty Rolls-Royce and Bentley cars disappeared into the sand during the Iraqi invasion. However, let us return to the supply of Phantom IVs and numerous other Phantom Vs & VIs. The first of these was coachbuilt by H.J. Mulliner and closely followed the design of the car supplied to Princess Elizabeth and HRH The Duke of Edinburgh without twin side-mounts and a glass section over the rear compartment. Design 7206 was a fairly upright body which was fitted with large ventilators to the sides and top of the scuttle and bonnet locks. Chassis 4AF 8 was described as a six-light saloon as it had no division although it was a very large car. The works at Chiswick eventually delivered the car to the Amir in July 1951.

Some four years later His Highness ordered another Phantom IV, but this time it was fitted with the slightly larger B81 6,515cc straight-eight engine and by now regular automatic transmission. It was virtually an identical copy of its predecessor and was given the design number 7376. This saloon, on chassis 4CS 2, was painted two-tone green with green upholstery and was fitted with air-conditioning originally supplied by the Chrysler Corporation. The car also sported three-inch wide front brakes. It was

BELOW, RIGHT, AND OVERLEAF: *Phantom V H.J.Mulliner, Park Ward limousine, on chassis 5LVF 123, delivered to the Amir of Kuwait in May 1967. It was equipped with air conditioning for the rear compartment, whitewall tyres and special indicator lamps on the crowns of the front wings.*

delivered in November 1955. The final Phantom IV to be supplied was chassis 4CS 4 which, like the previous Phantom IVs, was to a matching design 7376 and was fitted with all the usual detailing. This was handed over to The Amir in August 1955, thus completing the triumvirate.

Curiously, 4CS 4 was disposed of in the early sixties having covered only 1,700 miles on the 35 miles of road. The other two are still believed to be in the Amir's possession.

The Amir was succeeded on 1 January 1978 by the present ruler, Sheikh Jaber Al Ahmed Al Sabah. Before departing, he ordered a late series 1967 Phantom V. This was on chassis 5LVF 123, again to design 2003 lhd, and was delivered to the ruler in May 1967. Eventually this car came into the hands of a Californian collector just after it had completed some 50,000 miles, and nearly 1,200 miles could now be added to this on the odometer.

Unusually the Amir of Kuwait's Phantom V limousine, chassis 5LVF 123, had leather upholstery in the rear compartment. The veneered cocktail cabinet and occasional seats were a standard feature of design 2003.

The positions on both front wings where the Ruler's flags were flown can still be seen. In the last run before a GM 400 gearbox was added to the specification, PRX 4857 joined the stable. This lhd limousine was delivered in April 1977 and has a unique mascot. In place of the Flying Lady, the styling department at Crewe designed a special Rolls-Royce badge on a plinth to grace the radiator shell.

MALAYSIA

Malaysia became an independent state within the Commonwealth in August 1957. One of the curiosities of the Federation of Malaya has been the election of a King by the popular expedient of 'buggin's turn'. The last one to be crowned was the Sultan of Negri who was elevated on 26 April 1994. This 'election' is usually held every five years.

It is more than likely that the first Rolls-Royce to be provided for the Governor-General of Malaya was on a Phantom III chassis 3BT 193. This was delivered to Sir John Jarvis in June 1937, and acquired by the Viceroy of Malaya in 1946. It was bodied by Hooper, to their popular design 6273. The car was used until the early fifties, when it was withdrawn from service and returned to the UK to be replaced by a Park Ward limousine on chassis WHD 52. However, the then Governor-General (Viceroy), Sir Henry Gurney, who took over the Silver Wraith in June 1950, met disaster the following October, when he was assassinated in an ambush en route to a hill station in the limousine. Apparently, the escorting Land-Rover had broken down allowing the Rolls-Royce to proceed alone. The replacement limousine, possibly BLW 87, is not mentioned, although it is likely to have carried a Park Ward body.

One is certainly on firmer ground with an H.J. Mulliner limousine supplied to the supreme Ruler of the Federation of Malaya in July 1958. This was to design 7358 and included the following: built-in headlamps, refrigeration, a roof-mounted flag holder, emblazoned Grant of Arms on the doors, shields to front and rear and no number plates. One presumes this Silver Wraith chassis GLW 22, is still retained, although its precise whereabouts are not known.

In January 1963, the Sultan of Johore acquired an HJM, PW limousine, to design 2003 and on chassis 5VA 45. In August 1964, the State Secretary for Negri Sembilan obtained a Phantom V limousine, to design 2003, on Phantom V chassis 5VC 45 for the new King. In 1964, chassis 5VC 47 was also used by the State of Sabah.

In January 1968, the Sultan of Selangor took delivery of another Phantom V, this time on chassis 5VF 169. In December 1971 a Phantom VI chassis PRH 4668, with a Mulliner Park Ward limousine body, was then

The Ruler of the Federation of Malaysia's 1958 Silver Wraith
H.J. Mulliner-enclosed drive limousine, design 7358 on chassis GLW 22,
on ceremonial duty in 1963. The light colour no doubt helped
to reflect the heat.

purchased specifically for the King of Malaysia's personal use.

Possibly the most opulent was, however, a ceremonial State Landaulette on chassis GWH 10153 delivered to the Sultan of Selangor in 1986 and eventually used for the coronation celebrations of the new King in 1989. Since his term of office is not that far away, the Sultan's new car deserves rather more attention. The claret paintwork and black hood and roof were emphasised by the bright work; the crests on the doors were of

The bullet-holed Silver Wraith Park Ward limousine, chassis WHD 52, in which the Governor-General of Malaya, Sir Henry Gurney (inset left), was assassinated in 1950 by communist guerrillas led by Chin Peng (inset right). This is the only example of such a crime involving a Rolls-Royce.

24ct gold. The flag mountings on both wings were replaced by one single mounting placed behind the radiator. The interior was furnished in black leather at the front and beige leather to the rear, where there was full ceremonial fluorescent lighting and grab-handles to assist when standing upright. A TV was provided, along with a central cabinet with insulated flasks. Binocular storage and a radio-telephone eased one's passage through the crowds. As on other ceremonial State landaulettes, the rear seat could be raised hydraulically by about four inches. At the time, the completed landaulette was considered to be the ultimate in stately driving.

PAKISTAN

The Dominion of Pakistan came into being in 1947 following the Indian Independence Act, which advanced India and Pakistan to Dominion status in mid-August. The first Governor-General was Mahomed Ali Jinnah, *Quaid-i-Azam* – Great Leader – who had in 1916 been architect of the 'Lucknow Pact' between Muslim and Hindu, and later was instrumental in the creation of the new state, was sadly to die before the decade was out.

A Silver Wraith Hooper touring limousine was delivered to the first Governor-General of Pakistan which was finished in black with beige leather to front and rear and there was an instruction, it is claimed, that resin glue was to be used and not animal glue. Coconut fibre was substituted for horse-hair and kapok for ordinary down. Chassis WZB 7, to the Teviot design 8098, was handed over on 2 April 1948 and served the Governor-General until his death. In 1950 the touring limousine left the Head of State's ownership when it was acquired by the UK High Commissioner.

In 1956 Pakistan became a Republic under a Presidency. In 1967 the President ordered an H.J. Mulliner, Park Ward limousine (design 2003). Chassis 5VF 163 was handed over to the Head of State in December 1967. (However, within five years, the Pakistan government faced a dismemberment of the State, as rival factions vied for rule. East Pakistan was lost and Bangladesh was formally established in the spring of 1972.)

SAUDI ARABIA

In 1927, the kingdom of Hejaz and the sultanate of Nejd formed a union which is known today as the Kingdom of Saudi Arabia. The country comprises almost all of the Arabian peninsula, with the exception of the Republic of Yemen in the south and the United Arab Emirates. Today's population is estimated to be around 14,000,000.

Just prior to the Union of the two states, a Phantom I was ordered by The King of Hejaz. This was a Thrupp & Maberly cabriolet on chassis 66 TC and delivered in October 1926. However, in 1943 Churchill and Roosevelt met in Cairo and it was decided that King Ibn Saud would receive a DC3 aircraft as a gift from the Americans, and from British the gift of a … well, actually they had arrived with a canteen of cutlery! However, Churchill decided that the presentation of a Rolls-Royce would

The Phantom III Hooper cabriolet presented to King Ibn Saud in 1946 by the British Government., originally a Windovers limousine de ville on 1937 chassis 3CM 25. It was painted green because the King had been to Mecca.

*Elaborate interior of King Ibn Saud's Hooper cabriolet, chassis 3CM 25,
included a solid silver wash basin with water supply tank above, an electric fan,
silver-backed brushes and three vacuum flasks for iced water.*

be made in London after the war, as it was felt that the car represented the
best that Britain could produce. Unfortunately, nobody had pointed out to
Churchill that Rolls-Royce were still heavily engaged in war work and no
cars had been built since 1939. After a lot of desperate searching, a suitable
chassis was located – a choice of either a Windovers body or one by
Rippon. Eventually chassis 3CM 25 with a limousine de ville body by
Windovers was decided upon.

This chassis dated from 1937. Hooper & Co were still in the early
stages of returning to peacetime work in June 1945 and had just a handful
of employees to separate the body from the chassis. At this stage the
Phantom III running gear was sent up to Belper from London. This car and
the early Phantom IV chassis were the only ones worked on there, as post-
war production moved to Crewe. The eight year old chassis was overhauled
and had several modifications incorporated which included: the dropping
of the steering by two inches, exhaust-pipe re-routing, larger tyres for sand

grip, modified camshaft tappets, new road springs, larger capacity dynamo, a louvred bonnet and finally – a most troublesome alteration – an oil bath air filter to cope with sand and dust. This last item cost almost as much as a full-bodied Phantom III and had to be supported above the engine from several anchorage points.

Hooper & Co chose design 8021 which allowed for a four-door, all-weather. Legendary designer Osmond Rivers obtained the relevant pre-war chassis drawings from Derby. Chassis 3CM 25 was intended initially to have a full-air conditioning and an electric division. The unit was examined in a Northern Railway workshop, but this proved too bulky and thought was given to purchasing a Packard installation, but this was swiftly ruled out because it was manufactured in the US. Power operation to the main door windows was also considered, but this foundered because Hooper were unable to get a reliable system of routeing the cables through the door-jambs without trapping them. This was solved a year later by laying the cables in conduits. It had originally been thought that the King would sit cross-legged in the back and this had allowed Rolls-Royce to fit an extra chassis cross-member under the semi-circular seat. Later both had to be removed. The King's vehicle was painted in polychromatic dark green to the wings, mouldings, spare-wheel cover and discs and the remainder was in a lighter green. All cushioning had to be free of animal matter. The rear cabinet, which had to cope with tremendous heat, was made of a green met-alised finish and a special headlining was also included. The rear floor was covered with rubber underneath a felt overlay and on top of this a specially-dyed carpet was placed. The car was fitted with extra-wide running boards, complete with a set of handgrips on either side to assist those hanging on. Amongst the many extras were a Sterling silver ablution bowl, with water container above, front and rear heraldic decoration, silver-backed combs, thermos flasks, electric clock and a GEC 24-volt fan taken from an armoured vehicle and modified to run on 12 volts. Again, a problem arose over whether a radio receiver could be installed, but a suitable set was obtained from Philco & Co. Perhaps the most bizarre acquisitions were a siren and spotlight, which were eventually obtained from a Liverpool scrap-yard. The car was finally complete with its radiator-mounted flag mast and a full set of chassis and coachwork spares was supplied for shipment.

Despite the fact that this was Hooper's first post-war body and their craftsmen had been taken off priority aircraft work, the all-weather was completed some ten months after ordering, in February 1946. When the King's son Prince Faisal inspected the car, he pointed out that the King only sat cross-legged very rarely because of stiff knee-joints. Hooper then took an extra three weeks to put the seats back to normal, after which the car was shipped to the port of Jeddah. What happened after delivery? Well, in 1950, paint-patterns were requested following bodywork damage and some thirty years later the car returned for essential work at the Rolls-Royce London service centre, where it was said to be full of sand! After overhaul, it was sent back to Saudi Arabia.

A Phantom IV was supplied to Prince Talal of Saudi Arabia. This was on Chassis 4AF 22 and bodied by the French coachbuilder Franay which produced a particularly fine all-weather with twin sidemounts, face-forward seats, power windows and hood operation. The car was completed as a four-light with an electric division and was delivered in March 1952. It was returned to coachbuilders S.C. Gordon in the mid-eighties for remedial work to the body, which included renewing the piping to the front and off-side passenger seats.

In 1960, a body to design 980 by Park Ward was supplied on chassis 5LCG 3 and this was handed over in March 1962 to King Saud. In 1974, three more Phantom VIs, PRX 4803 and PRX 4809, were delivered. These were normal MPW limousines and were joined in 1975 by an earlier sister car, PRX 4802, which was heavily armour-plated, as was PRX 4856 delivered in August 1978. Four more Phantom VIs have also been finished for Prince Fahad (PRX 4633), Prince Talal (PRH 4713), Prince Mohammed (PRH 4828) and Prince Sultan bin Abed al-Aziz (PRX 4869).

SINGAPORE

In 1946, The Straits Settlements became the State of Singapore and received independence in 1959 as part of the Federation of Malaya. Seven years later, Singapore became an independent city/state within the Commonwealth and has remained so right up to the present day. The population today is about three million. In 1926 (just after the introduction

Barker open-drive landaulette on 20hp chassis, GUK 51, for Sir
Laurence Guillemard, Governor of Singapore. It was delivered in August
1926. Note the louvred 'colonial' bonnet and rear-mounted spare wheel.

of four-wheel brakes), an order was placed by the then Governor for a
Barker landaulette. This was on 20hp chassis GUK 51. A 'colonial bonnet'
was specified, along with a crown to front and rear and cyphers on the two
main doors.

After the recovery of Singapore in 1946, the Colonial Office looked
around for a suitable and impressive limousine. As luck would have it, a
suitable Hooper body was located and the limousine, to design 6443, was
shipped out where it became the official transport in late 1946. The
Phantom III chassis 3BT 97 was destined to remain as the Governor's car
until being replaced in 1954.

In August 1953, Hooper & Co had been approached about a replacement landaulette and hoped to be favoured with the work of building the
body, regardless of chassis. In October 1953, they submitted specification
983 on a Silver Wraith lwb chassis to the authorities.

The landaulette, on chassis BLW 92, was to design 8403 and featured
the standard holder above the windscreen, an internal telephone, a radio-

TOP, AND ABOVE: *The Governor of Singapore acquired Phantom III 3BT 97 in 1946. It had been built as a Hooper limousine, design 6443, for A.F. Bassett and was originally delivered in June 1937.*

This telephoto view of the Governor of Singapore's 1954 Silver Wraith, chassis BLW 92, disguises its 17ft 2in length. The Hooper landaulette body, no. 10008, to design 8403 was a one-off on the Silver Wraith chassis.

telephone, crowns to the front and rear, a hinged centre armrest to rear with a lockable lid and finally a system which enabled the Governor's companion to receive a cool blast from an electric fan situated over the division. The English Royal Arms were painted on both main doors and the chassis was returned from Hooper & Co to be strengthened; the rear springs were changed too.

The complete weight was just over 46cwt and the car was tested over a distance of eighty miles before being shipped to Government House on 7 August 1954. Having covered something around 50,000 miles, the Hooper

ABOVE: *The President of Singapore's Phantom V H.J.Mulliner, Park Ward*
limousine, chassis 5VF 31, on royal duties.
RIGHT: *The Governor of Ceylon's 1925 Phantom I landaulette, chassis 101 MC,*
transports the Duke of Gloucester.

landaulette later went to Germany and then to the United Kingdom where
a further 38,000 miles have been recorded.

Finally, in June 1966, a Phantom V, chassis 5 VF 31, to the standard
limousine design 2003 was delivered to the President of Singapore.

SRI LANKA

Ceylon came under British rule with the Treaty of Kandy in 1816.
The island was granted Dominion status in 1948 and ruled by a
Governor-General. In May 1972, the country adopted a republi-
can constitution. Today's population is estimated to be 15,000,000.

Ceylon's involvement with Rolls-Royce probably goes back as far as

H.R.H. The
Duke of
Gloucester
arriving at
Government
Lodge
Colombo

The Duke of Gloucester arriving
at King's Pavilion, Kandy, Ceylon

LEFT, AND ABOVE: *Now awaiting restoration in Alaska, Silver Wraith WYA 1 with H.J. Mulliner sedanca de ville coachwork had a distinguished past in Ceylon. The timber-framed body was covered with light alloy panels. Note the traditional right-hand gearchange for the manual gearbox.*

the purchase of a Phantom I which was one of the very first sanctions, that is within the first 100 allocated, of chassis 101 MC. Barker were instructed to complete a State landaulette for delivery in the middle of the year and, indeed, it arrived there in May 1925. The limousine had twin spare wheels on either side of the bonnet, crowns to front and rear, with rear door-mounted cyphers. Blue wing-mounted sidelights completed the specification. The vehicle was probably in use for over a decade.

In 1947, H.E. The Governor-General, Lord Soulbury, acquired two Rolls-Royce cars of the Silver Wraith type. The first, chassis WVA 40, was fitted with a Hooper touring limousine body to design 8034, their first post-war Silver Wraith concept, and finished in maroon with beige leather throughout. This was delivered in December 1947.

The second car was an H.J. Mulliner sedanca de ville to design 7055 which more than likely travelled out with the touring limousine on the *S.S. Clan Maclennan* from Birkenhead to Colombo. This was also maroon with

159

Her Majesty The Queen alights from the Silver Wraith H.J. Mulliner
sedanca de ville, chassis WYA 1, in June 1954 outside the new
Parliament building of the independent dominion of Ceylon.

beige upholstery and had an oil-bath air cleaner. In the latter case the
guarantee became effective for the Chassis WYA 1 from the 6th
January 1948. Amidst great splendour, Her Majesty The Queen opened
Parliament in April 1954 and entered a magnificent building which was
completely open to the public from end to end. In the late 1950s it is more
than likely that chassis WYA 1 was sold back to the United Kingdom, where
it acquired the number plate SXX 731, issued by the Greater London
Council. Today it is the subject of restoration in Alaska.

THAILAND

Thailand became a constitutional monarchy in 1932 and the present King succeeded his brother in June, 1946 to become King Bhumibol. Today's population is around 56 million.

In all likelihood, the first car delivered to the then Prince Regent was a Hooper Silver Ghost chassis 108 AG. This was a 1921 chassis and carried the special mascot of the Kings of Thailand (formerly Siam), depicting a Garuda. This was followed in late 1930 by Phantom III chassis 178 GY with a most unusual body by the French coachbuilder Saoutchik who provided a limousine for the monarch. In 1935, 20/25hp chassis GLG 38 with

Silver Ghost, chassis 108 AG, with Hooper cabriolet coachwork
delivered to the Prince Regent of Siam (now Thailand) in 1921.
Electric lighting and starting were standard but only the rear
wheels were braked.

*H.J. Mulliner termed this body on the King of Thailand's Phantom III,
chassis 3DL 158, a limousine de ville. The roof over the driving compartment could be opened. Note the slim screen pillars and special mascot.*

a body by Hooper found its way to the Royal Court. Just before the war,
a Phantom III was shipped from Southampton on chassis 3DL 158, and
this was an H.J. Mulliner-bodied car with a sedanca de ville style, which
was then used by the Prince Regent up until his succession by the present
King in 1946. At the time of completion, it was fitted with a single side-
mounted spare and an offside-mounted flag mast.

It was not until many years later that the King decided to acquire
another Phantom. This was in 1973, when he obtained Phantom VIs PRH
4765 and PRH 4767 followed by the armour-plated PGH 115 in 1980. He
has also taken possession of one Silver Shadow II (chassis 30019), two other
Silver Spur IIs (MCH 32592 & 32595) and a 1990 Corniche III. The latter, chassis LCH 30285, is used only once a year for Trooping the Colour.

UNITED ARAB EMIRATES

Comprising Abu Dhabi, Ajman, Ummal Qaiwain, Dubai, Fujeirah, Ras al Khaimah and Sharjah, the United Arab Emirates currently has a population of 1,600,000. The seven Emirates proceeded to independence individually. The principal emirate is Abu Dhabi, where gas and oil revenues make an enormous contribution. The output of the oil-fields was estimated to be around one-and-a-half million barrels a day in 1989. As Qatar and Dubai were to be members of the UAE, but chose independence, it would seem only sensible to group the former Trucial States together.

Qatar received its first Rolls-Royce in January 1952 and this was a limousine by Park Ward to design 146 on chassis WOF 46. Exactly two years later, The Ruler of Qatar received a Hooper touring limousine to design 8390 on chassis LBLW 57. Originally LBLW 57 had been intended for the Iraq Petroleum Company but this was soon transferred to the Ruler of Qatar. The touring limousine was finished in black pearl and grey side panels and maroon leather throughout. It had been intended for the Brussels Show, but in the circumstances ended up in Iraq in November 1954. Anything the Ruler of Qatar could do, the Ruler of Abu Dhabi could also do, and in January 1966 he took delivery of 5VE 15, an H.J. Mulliner Park Ward limousine.

AFRICA

CENTRAL AFRICAN REPUBLIC

Jean Bedel Bokassa, the president and then (from 1977) self-styled emperor of the Central African Republic, ordered a long wheelbase Silver Shadow in early 1975. By all accounts, it lacked nothing in its specification, even down to a boot-fitted refrigerator and tinted windows. One of the more important additions was a flagmast which was attached to the lhd car between the overrider and the inside headlamp. The car joined the state fleet in the summer of 1975 and the guarantee card was issued for chassis LRX 22245 to run for three years. In the early 1980s the car came into the possession of the manager of a hotel in Sursee, Switzerland. The last mention of the lwb Silver Shadow in the membership list shows it to still be in the possession of the proprietor.

LEFT, AND ABOVE: *Long wheelbase Silver Shadow, LRX 22245, supplied to Emperor Bokassa in 1975. The black Everflex-covered roof, smaller rear window and longer rear door window (to allow for the 4in longer wheelbase) were standard features. The car was no doubt used by the Emperor during his incredibly expensive coronation, in 1977, but not when he went to trial in 1988.*

165

EGYPT

The Kingdom of Egypt came into being when a British Protectorate lapsed in February 1922 and King Fuad was proclaimed monarch. The dynasty, so quickly established, was to last just thirty years and had three Kings. During this time, seven cars appear to have been ordered from the Derby works.

The first such chassis was 12 YB, a 1914 series of the renowned Silver Ghost, probably acquired in the inter-war years. The Rothschild landaulette was still in service some thirty years later and had, in all likelihood, been in the original ownership of King Fuad whose cypher appears on the rear doors. The Silver Ghosts were not fitted with front wheel brakes until 1925, and is clearly shown in a 1946 photograph.

Hooper & Co were responsible for the supply of the first car ordered directly by King Fuad just after the announcement of the new Phantom series in May of 1925. This was an-open drive limousine mounted on chassis 118 HC. Certainly in profile it gave an appearance not unlike those cars supplied to the British Royal Family, who of course patronised the same coachbuilder. There were several modifications, however. To accommodate the extreme heat of the Egyptian summer, the bonnet was fitted with louvres which ran the entire length from radiator to scuttle. A speaking tube was installed for communication with the driver and heraldic decoration was added to the rear doors. The completed vehicle was delivered to Alexandria and issued with its guarantee card in February 1926.

When the 20/25hp Rolls-Royce was announced in 1929, King Fuad ordered a chassis of this type. GLR 62 was on the lengthened 132in wheelbase chassis and was finished as an enclosed limousine. This impressive vehicle was allocated design number 4495; this single design number was issued to the drawing office in May 1930 and, presumably, the completed car was handed over in late autumn of that year.

Chassis 22 OR was in the last series for the Phantom I (as it subsequently became) and was ordered from Hooper & Co early in 1929. Designed as a landaulette on a lwb chassis, it sported twin spare wheels to either side of the scuttle, and a rear luggage grid which accommodated the normal luggage load of up to three or four people. The final testing at Hooper was in mid-September 1929 and the car was shipped to Alexandria

Hooper's official photograph of the open-drive limousine, body no. 6449, built to the order of King Fuad of Egypt on Phantom I chassis 118 HC. Note the louvred bonnet and the speaking tube trumpet just behind the chauffeur's head.

towards the end of that month, with the journey time taking a little over a week. The guarantee card was issued shortly afterwards.

This smart car had been in use less than a year before it was joined by a Phantom II on chassis 30 GY. Again, a long-type chassis was specified, coupled to a louvred bonnet, and twin forward-mounted spare wheels. The limousine design (4437) was never to be repeated and the completed car was tested at the coachbuilders in early October 1930 and guaranteed from the 25th of that month.

Curiously, in 1934 the Egyptian King rebodied a Silver Ghost of decidedly ancient vintage (1915) in his fleet. Chassis 31 ED was referred to in the Hooper archives as an 'old 40/50'. It was completed as an enclosed limousine with new bonnet and delivered in the spring of 1934.

With the advent of the V-12 series in 1935, King Fuad decided to order a Phantom III and this was on Chassis 3 CM 63. This was another enclosed limousine with a louvred bonnet, the louvres set at an angle of 11 degrees. Other modifications included spare wheel carriers on either side of the bonnet, a long-plate clutch, headlamps which dipped to offside and both speedometer and petrol gauge showing miles and kilometres. The guarantee was in force from 20 January 1938.

King Fuad was succeeded by King Farouk, who ordered a second Phantom III – one only fifteen from the end of production – in late 1939. Chassis 3DL 182 was delivered to the coachbuilders Charlesworth in Coventry. The reasons for a change of coachbuilder are not clear, but it is possible that the Hooper workforce was already building aluminium frames for the Royal Air Force by this time. This final car was supplied with a radio, built-in heater, the usual louvred bonnet, provision for a rear compartment speedometer, double filament headlamps and, quite importantly, a special petrol filter. Probably the most sensational addition was the supply of power-operated windows. Divisions had had this facility since the mid-1930s, but the opening of doors meant a new treatment to conduct the electric supply to the windows. The car was finished in royal red with black wings, wheels and roof. The car was handed over to the shippers in early April 1940, and the guarantee became effective just a week later.

The fate of the two latter Phantoms is to some extent wrapped in secrecy. 3 CM 63 was still in Cairo in the mid-'50s, but the Charlesworth Phantom, chassis 3DL 182, was shipped to Austria in 1992 and is now known to be undergoing a major restoration. It seems likely that if one Phantom III survived, others may also be around and we will have to wait and see if they are discovered.

ETHIOPIA

From his accession in 1930 to his deposition in 1974, apart from a period in exile from 1936 to 1941, Emperor Haile Selassie was the Ethiopian Head of State. A Rolls-Royce enthusiast, he kept several models at Addis Ababa, ranging from the mighty Phantom II to the impressive Silver Wraith.

Haile Selassie's predecessor, Negus Tafari, had ordered an open-drive landaulette on chassis 6 XJ from coachbuilders Hooper & Co. Because of the intense heat, especially during summer months, the chassis was equipped with full-length bonnet louvres. There were twin spare wheels on either side of the bonnet, polished aluminium wheel discs and, very unusually, an extension seat beyond the rear chassis frame to support a pair of warriors. With everyone on board there must have been quite a load over the rear axle. The completed drawings were passed to the Hooper staff in September 1929. The completed car was handed over to the shippers around Christmas time and the guarantee card was issued in January 1930. Within the year, Haile Selassie succeeded.

The Emperor was in exile during the manufacturing period of the V-12 Phantom III, and when he returned in 1941, Rolls-Royce was solely concerned with the war effort. After the cessation of hostilities, the company concentrated its efforts on the Silver Wraith model. The Emperor may well have considered the moderate wheelbase of 10ft 7ins to be rather small, and it was not until the advent of the 6in longer wheelbase that he decided again to patronise Rolls-Royce.

This time his Imperial Majesty chose a series of three Silver Wraith chassis. The first to arrive in Addis Ababa was chassis CLW 36, a splendid

BELOW: *Unique open-drive landaulette with rumble seat behind built by Hooper & Co on 1929 Phantom I, chassis 6 XJ, for the King of Abyssinia (Ethiopia). Note the polished aluminium bonnet and wheel cover.*
FOLLOWING PAGES: *1954 Silver Wraith Park Ward landaulette, on chassis CLW 36, built for Haile Selassie of Ethiopia.*

looking Park Ward-bodied landaulette which sported whitewall tyres, Victoria maroon metallic (as on all the Palace cars and provided originally by General Motors), and a roof-mounted illuminated heraldic shield with a flagmast to its rear. Park Ward only built two landaulettes to this design (the other for the Governor of the Gold Coast) and it was numbered design 558. The rear boot was rather high mounted and tended to give the car an unfortunate rear aspect, and certainly prevented the head leather from folding down neatly. Rather more fortunate was a larger rear window which certainly gave drivers a better backwards view. The completed car was delivered to Addis Ababa and guaranteed in September 1954.

The second Silver Wraith, chassis DLW 82, was fitted with the larger 4,887cc six-cylinder engine and was built to design 7348 by H.J. Mulliner. This was essentially a touring limousine without extra seats, but harbouring an electric division, picnic tables and a headroom of 48.5 inches. As on the previous vehicle, the heraldic shield was roof-mounted with provision for flying the standard behind. The paint scheme was as before. The car was issued with its guarantee in February 1955.

In July 1958, Hooper & Co received an enquiry for the provision of a four-door convertible, again to be based on the Silver Wraith chassis. Curiously breaking with tradition, the Emperor decided to have a lhd car and this came through as LHLW 51. The ceremonial all-weather bodywork was the same as that provided for the pair to be sent to Australia and cost £4,250, less 20%. As with all cars for the antipodes, the all-weather was to design 8548 and whitewall tyres were insisted upon. Included in the specification for body 10290 was an electric division, face-forward seating meeting in the centre and power operated windows. The hood was semi-concealed with a matching hood bag and chromium-plated hood irons. As on the Australian ceremonial all-weathers, the headlamps were recessed into the nose of the front wings, an arrangement which attempted to minimise the upward throw of light beams. The rear compartment's fold-down centre armrest held a looking glass plus two silver-topped perfume bottles. Also fitted was a detachable full-width handrail which ran the length of the division. No numberplates were required. A Radiomobile electric wing aerial was fitted; the twin radio sets caused some consternation and were eventually fitted (a pair of 230 Rs) in short and medium wave. One was under the control of the driver and the other from the nearside seat

Emperor Haile Selassie (in dark suit) alights from the Silver Wraith H.J.
Mulliner touring limousine on chassis DLW 82. The coachbuilders actually
called this design, 7348, a sports limousine. It was delivered in 1955.

armrest. A speaker was fitted under the dashboard and a pair behind
the division.

Progress continued on the all-weather and this included the supply of
a set of raised metal crests fixed through boltholes to the rear door panels.
The charges for this were £31.50 a pair. Hooper must have been extremely
pleased when they received the costings – for handling the arrangements
they simply doubled their price. This system also applied to the provision
of a flagstaff which was topped by a Crown. Spinks' account to Hooper &
Co shows a cost of £75 which was billed as £144. Not surprisingly, this was
turned down at the last minute and the unit made locally! Curiously, on the
only picture I can locate of the all-weather, the crown can just be seen atop

This ornate crown, made in Ethiopia, topped the flagmast on Emperor Haile Selassie's Silver Wraith Hooper allweather on chassis LHLW 51.

the flagmast. Two other masts were also fitted on the crowns of the front wings. Owing to the extraordinary amount of additional work, the car was two months late and delivery was finally effected on 20 April 1959.

There is a mystery surrounding the possible supply of a Phantom VI in 1974. This was supposedly PRH 4791 which boasted only a four light configuration. However, considering that the Selassie regime ended in that year, and the picture shows a Phantom with doors arranged according to the federal safety specification (hinged at the front) this is, I think, extremely unlikely. Also, Rolls-Royce records show that PRH 4791 was Coffee Bean Brown and supplied to a UK customer on 14 June 1974.

Finally, what happened to the Phantom II and the Silver Wraiths? I sent a letter concerning the matter to the Ethiopian First Secretary (information) and received the reply: "Chairman Mengistu, I am told, has personally used the Silver Wraith, but I have personally never seen him in it. No further information is available."

The Queen and Duke of Edinburgh ride in the Silver Wraith Hooper all-weather, chassis LHIW 51, on a visit to Ethiopia. Note the crown surmounting the flagmast and the hooded headlamps, the latter a Hooper speciality.

GABON

The Republic of Gabon lies on the Atlantic coast at the Equator and this enclave of just over a million inhabitants covers an area of around 100,000 square miles. In 1960, Gabon became fully independent and in 1967 President Albert Bongo was elected to rule. Over the subsequent years he has been re-elected by his countrymen, although a multi-party system was adopted in 1990.

Despite the moderate size of the republic, the President has owned four Phantom VIs. The first purchase was in 1971, when His Excellency ordered a lhd Phantom on chassis **PRX 4664**. In those days, before European safety regulations, the doors were hinged front and rear. The car was delivered in mid-1972.

The second chassis allocated was **PRH 4716** and was, unusually,

President Albert-Bernard Bongo of Gabon watches the operation of the hood on a Silver Shadow drophead coupé while visiting Rolls-Royce Ltd. On the right is Roger Cra'ster who looked after Rolls-Royce VIP sales.

a ceremonial State Landaulette. By this time, the European safety regulations were in force. These required burst-proof locks, a collapsible steering column and a far stronger handbrake. There was also a requirement to drive the vehicle into a 100 ton block, which took two attempts to get right. The car was delivered in 1972.

The final two Phantom VI cars were delivered around 1976. These were chassis PRX 4844 and PRX 4845 and both were armoured limousines. Whether any of the cars survive is a matter for speculation.

GHANA

The decision was announced in the mid-fifties by the then British Colonial Secretary to grant independence to the African colony. In March 1957, Ghana (known up until then as The Gold Coast) received full sovereignty and became a member of the British Commonwealth.

Until this time, the Head of State – the Governor – and later the President (following the introduction of a Republican Constitution) used Rolls-Royce limousines. The first of these was a Silver Wraith, chassis number ALW 32, which was given a landaulette style of coachwork. H.J. Mulliner were responsible for the body and the chassis was delivered to the Chiswick company in late August 1952. This special body was equipped with an oil-bath air cleaner, blue roof identification light, gilt crowns to front and rear number plates and with a black landaulette head to the rear compartment. It was finished in black all over, with beige leather at the front of the interior and fawn cloth to the rear. The completed landaulette was tested in mid-December 1952 and after the festive season was shipped to Takoradi where the guarantee card was issued on 24 February 1953. This was one of two such creations to design 7281. However, two years later, the landaulette was damaged in rioting in Kumasi in March 1955 and the decision was made to return the car to the Chiswick works of H.J. Mulliner for repair. Many years later, the car (in a somewhat sorry state) was put up for sale in South London and is believed to have been acquired by a Spanish purchaser in 1988.

Silver Wraith supplied to the Governor of The Gold Coast in 1953.
Chassis ALW 32 was bodied by H.J. Mulliner who termed this design
(7281) a pullman landaulette. Note the blue police lamp and height of
the folded landaulette hood.

The replacement vehicle on chassis DLW 126 was a Park Ward-bodied creation and was one of two; the other went to the Emperor of Ethiopia. Unlike the previous landaulette, this was constructed entirely out of alloy and was in place by July 1955. Interestingly, in 1957, another Park Ward landaulette arrived on chassis FLW 61 with twin carburettors, power steering and a larger 4,887cc engine. This was the later 727 design, with an improved rear aspect. The car was delivered to the Government Transport Department, Ghana in January 1957. It probably shared the journey over with chassis FLW 72, a true touring limousine by H.J. Mulliner with an electric division between front and rear compartments.

In November 1961 it was announced that Her Majesty The Queen would visit Accra and outlying areas of the new Republic. The accompanying print shows President Nkrumah with The Queen in an H.J. Mulliner designed open convertible with the chassis number SGE 310, delivered in September 1958. The drophead boasted a radiator mounted flag mast and just in front of the bumper was a colourful Grant of Arms. It is followed by the two Park Ward-bodied Silver Wraith landaulettes.

HM The Queen is accompanied by President Nkrumah of Ghana in the 1958 Silver Cloud H.J. Mulliner drophead coupé on chassis SGE 310, built to design 7410.

KENYA

The Republic of Kenya came into being in 1963, having chosen Jomo Kenyatta as its head of state. He was succeeded in 1978 by President Arap Moi.

President Kenyatta was reputedly a modest man who probably preferred a rather less ostentatious mode of transport. However, in early 1963, the President was aware that a new Phantom V had been ordered for his use. In the previous October, H.J. Mulliner, Park Ward had successfully redesigned their Phantom V from the Park Ward design 980 to that of H.J. Mulliner, Park Ward Design 2003. This incorporated chromium-plated brass window frames, double headlamps and a redesigned boot. Less apparent was the Silver Cloud III engine with 7% more available power.

The government of Kenya was supplied with chassis 5VA 95 which had been ordered by London dealers H.R. Owen for stock. The Phantom V was shipped in early Autumn 1963 with the car receiving its guarantee card in November of that year. I am told that the Phantom has received only very moderate use and is unlikely to have covered more than 10,000 miles during the last thirty-odd years. The car has been kept at the old Government House Garage in Nairobi, where it remains today.

LIBERIA

Liberia was established in 1822 and recognised as an independent state in 1847. For many years the President was William Tubman who ordered a most opulent Rolls-Royce limousine before his demise almost a quarter of a century ago.

This was ordered at the end of 1962 and was to the new design 2003 on chassis 5LVA 37. What distinguished the car were the twin flag masts which were set into the front wings and the air-conditioning fitted into the rear compartment. The photograph (overleaf) was taken just after completion, in Merrington Road, London. Soon afterwards, in May 1963, the car was delivered to the President of Liberia and the guarantee card was issued at the same time.

It is not known if, after over thirty years, the limousine survives and in what state. Enquiries to date have not so far elicited any details.

LIBYA

Perhaps Libya's principal claim to fame is that it was the first State to be created by a resolution of the United Nations Assembly, in 1951. The monarch was King Idris, a member of the Sanusi tribe, who was overthrown in a bloodless coup in 1969. Today the population numbers around four and a half million.

The only Rolls-Royce delivered to His Majesty was a lhd Phantom V with coachwork by Park Ward on chassis 5LCG 53. This was again to design 980 and was made near the end of the run of this style. Just thirteen chassis remained to be bodied by coachbuilders Park Ward and James Young before the second series began in September 1962. Representatives of His Majesty King Idris received the Phantom in April 1962. It is not known if the car survives.

MALAWI

Formerly known as Nyasaland, Malawi became a Republic some two years after achieving independence from Britain in 1966. Today's population is close to the eight million mark. Dr Hastings Banda was elected in 1966 and sworn in as President for life in 1971. He was still in office over twenty years later.

The FLW series of Silver Wraith was introduced in October 1956 and boasted optional power steering and twin SU carburettors. By the time chassis FLW 60 was built, a higher compression ratio of 8:1 was available and power-assisted steering had become a usual fitment. Chassis FLW 75

FOLLOWING PAGES: *H.J. Mulliner, Park Ward Phantom V limousine, chassis 5LVA 37, supplied to the President of Liberia in 1963. Note the massive flagmasts and the rear aerial for the radio-telephone.*

was fitted with a Park Ward landaulette body and, rather curiously, blue front sidelights were supplied. As on other colonial landaulettes being built at the time, a facility was provided for flying a flag from the roof. The completed vehicle was handed over to the Governor in March 1957.

Five RHD design 727s were supplied to Colonial and Commonwealth governments. The sixth (LHD) went to the Queen of the Netherlands. It is claimed that HM Queen Elizabeth, the Queen Mother, used FLW 75 at one time; if so it was probably during a visit to Nyasaland in the early 1960s. Today the car has been fitted with air-conditioning, as a result of its sojourn in the United States, and the mileage is around 73,000. The vehicle has

LEFT, AND ABOVE: *Silver Wraith Park Ward landaulette delivered to the Governor of Malawi in 1957 on chassis FLW 75. This was based on Park Ward's limousine design 551. Note unusual rear lamps and blue front sidelamps.*

again crossed the Atlantic and today it is part of a Dutch collection.

A lwb Silver Cloud III with four-door coachwork was ordered by Dr Banda. As with the Australian duo, CDL 3 was fitted with single headlamps and delivered in 1964. Curiously, H.J. Mulliner had originally provided such a car to an American, Louis Marx & Co, on the Silver Cloud II chassis (LLCB 16) and the merged firms of H.J. Mulliner, Park Ward were happy to repeat the order. Eventually they were to supply five more of the four-door cabriolets. In 1968, the Government of Malawi ordered a Phantom V limousine with coachwork by H.J. Mulliner, Park Ward on chassis 5VF 181. Delivered in June 1968 it was the penultimate Phantom V chassis before the introduction of the Phantom VI in October.

Despite many pleas to the Malawi High Commission, I cannot report any progress on enquiries as to the survival of the last two chassis.

MOROCCO

Following a joint declaration between France and Spain in 1956, Morocco became an independent state under the Sultan of Morocco, who later adopted the title King Mohammed V. He was succeeded in February 1961 by King Hassan II.

A trait of Rolls-Royce customers was that quite a few who patronised a particular coachbuilder were often content to remain with that firm, and so it was with King Mohammed who was happy to remain with James Young for three series of vehicles. The monarch was possibly influenced by the legendary socialite Barbara Hutton, who in the fifties mentioned that negotiating the Casbah in her Rolls-Royce often resulted in scrapes on either side. Wisely, His Majesty arranged to have the entrances to the Casbah widened. (Incidentally, the Duke of Gloucester's James Young Phantom V was also rather wide and negotiating the garden entrance at Buckingham Palace had to be attempted rather delicately, as it was less than three inches wider!)

The first limousine the new King ordered was chassis LF LW 80 which was one of fifteen seven-seater limousines to design WRM 35S. This had the by now obligatory built-in headlamps, 49-inch interior height and doors hinged to the front (the first few limousines had doors hinged forward and aft). This was the final Silver Wraith limousine design from James Young, and the completed car was handed over in March 1957.

In late 1963, King Hassan II decided to order a Silver Cloud III on a lwb chassis, LCDL 1, to design SCT 200. This was only a two-car design and was fitted with just two doors, albeit on a lwb chassis. Since the King's vehicle had a flagmast on either side of the two wings, it was certainly very distinctive. The Silver Cloud was also fitted with tinted glass to the front, which usually indicated the presence of air-conditioning. The car was delivered to Rabat in April 1964.

The final limousine to be ordered was a superb touring model to design PV 22 requested in the autumn of 1962. This was chassis 5LVA 41 and James Young were able to produce the car for test in the new year, and deliver it in February 1963. Like all touring limousines, it was fitted with a sideways-facing occasional seat and superb cabinet work to the rear of the division. With less seating space required inside, it was quite possible to allow for a steeper rake to the back, thus giving the impression of lowering the roof.

Sadly, the millionairess Barbara Hutton died in the late sixties, and one suspects that it was with some relief that the King could begin to order cars with a more modest pedigree!

NIGERIA

The Federal Republic of Nigeria on the West Coast of Africa has a population of just around 110,000,000. In the past, Colonial Governors would very often draw their official transport from either Armstrong-Siddeley, Daimler, Humber and only occasionally from Rolls-Royce. By the early fifties, however, there was a preference for the latter manufacturer. A Daimler Straight-Eight was supplied for the use of the

Hooper's landaulette design 8445 for the Governor of Nigeria's Silver Wraith ELW 55.

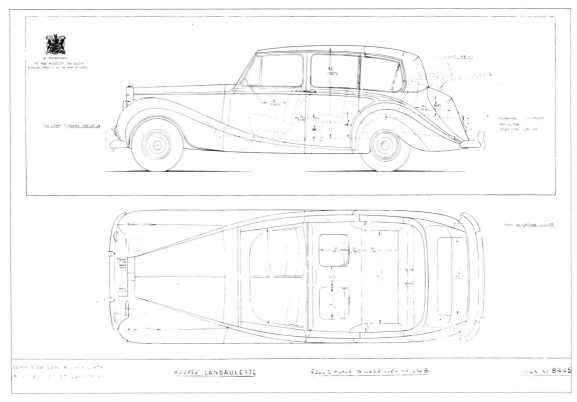

Governor-General in September 1950 (chassis 51723). It had covered only 7,000 miles, but was shipped back to the UK in 1952/3 for remedial work.

In May 1952, a special lwb cabriolet with a power-operated hood was delivered to the renowned Rolls-Royce purchaser Nubar Gulbenkian. The open car was quite obviously overweight and Rolls-Royce considered the vehicle on the borderline as regards passing it off test. Chassis ALW 11, to design 8335, was adopted for Head of State use more by accident than design. Mr Gulbenkian was obviously not happy with the car and sold it back to Hooper & Co just two years later, as they had agreed to have it back should it be unsatisfactory. Mr Gulbenkian already had a sedanca de ville which was issued with its guarantee card in August 1953. Hooper & Co found a buyer in the Nigerian colony and the open four-door cabriolet was quickly turned around and sent out to Nigeria. Originally the car was painted two-tone but was repainted black, with a shield fitment to the front and flag-standard to the offside, by Hooper & Co in 1954. The lucky recipient was Sir Bryan Sharwood-Smith, the then Governor of Northern Nigeria. The purchase of a landaulette for use by the Governor was obviously inspired by The Queen's decision to bring out Rolls-Royce Ltd.'s Phantom IV Hooper landaulette, chassis 4BP 5. This car was acquired in 1959 from the company, and in recent years has been retired to The Queen's Sandringham Motor Museum. Incidentally, two Silver Cloud saloons were also shipped out for the tour.

The Silver Wraith, chassis ELW 55, was ordered from Hooper & Co in the autumn of 1955. The bodywork style was that of a landaulette and the rear interior body height was 52 inches. The car was finished in black with a leather hood over the rear compartment, crests on the rear doors and detachable flagstaffs on the wings. It was furnished in brown upholstery, with illuminated shields to front and rear, two interior fans at either end of the division top rail, loose covers, a blue police light to the roof, a mohair rug to the rear and an oil-bath air cleaner. The State landaulette went on test on 14 April 1956 and the completed vehicle was issued with its guarantee card on 1 May on arrival in Lagos. The Governor-General, Sir James Robertson, was the recipient.

The Governor of Western Nigeria, Sir John Rankine, had taken delivery of chassis ELW 4 in October 1955. This was a Park Ward limousine which had been ordered the previous spring. It was probably the car that

*Unusual grey and black colour scheme on Silver Wraith chassis HLW 35
delivered to the Governor of Western Nigeria in December 1958. The
Hooper landaulette coachwork was to design 8445 and included a blue
police lamp and flag mountings. It is now in Hong Kong and has been
altered to include a television and air conditioning.*

failed to proceed at Kaduna whilst on the Royal Tour of 1956, but this did not prevent Sir John from ordering a landaulette from Hooper & Co in the late spring of 1958. Chassis HLW 35 was again to the design 8445 and had been originally designed with a slim rear quarter-light which was later omitted from production. The car proceeded through the works as the previous accepted design for a State landaulette, but actually to the specification 1021. The colour scheme adopted was the roof, front and rear wings in black and shell grey to the bonnet top and sides. The interior was grey leather. ELW 4 was used during independence celebrations attended by HRH The Duke of Gloucester and HRH The Princess Alice on 1 October 1960. As the Governor-General probably used the car on a visit to the West, one should perhaps mention that the extras included a blue identification light on the front of the roof, English Royal Arms on the doors with Crowns front and rear, shield covers, and flag staffs to offside front wing and also behind the identification light. Inside were two fans at the top of the division rail and, rather specially, two thermos flasks and glasses were fitted into the rear cabinet. Perhaps the installation of a Halda speed pilot on the front

ABOVE: *Sir John Rankine's 1955 Silver Wraith Park Ward limousine on chassis ELW 4. Note the crown above the bumper, blue police lamp and absence of a radiator mascot.*
LEFT, AND FOLLOWING PAGES: *1956 Silver Wraith Hooper landaulette, body 10176, on chassis ELW 55 for the Governor-General of Nigeria. The built-in headlamps were then a new styling feature.*

of the glove-compartment ensured the Governor's appointments were kept on time. This vehicle was the last Rolls-Royce to be delivered in the colonial period, but the new Government of Nigeria continued to use the Crewe company for many years to come.

The first post-independence car was 5AT 72, to design 980, and was delivered to the Governor of Northern Nigeria in autumn 1960. In February 1965, a Phantom V landaulette, design 2047, was provided for the use of the government of East Nigeria on chassis 5DV 41. Two other Phantoms for regional Premiers were also supplied.

What happened to the Silver Wraiths and Phantoms? Well, in chronological terms: the Silver Wraith cabriolet ALW 11 was last heard to

ABOVE: *The ex-Gulbenkian Silver Wraith cabriolet, ALW 11, used by The Queen on a State visit to Nigeria.*
RIGHT, TOP: *The Hooper cabriolet, ALW 11, was ideal for those with tall formal headgear. Note the faired-in headlamps with Perspex covers.*
RIGHT, BOTTOM: *Phantom V landaulette, design 2047, on chassis 5VD 41 after shipment for restoration in 1993.*

be still in Kaduna, chassis ELW 55 has completed just 30,000 miles and was repatriated to Great Britain to be restored in the late sixties; ELW 4 has unfortunately disappeared but HLW 35 survives having been returned to the United Kingdom in 1977 – it underwent restoration in 1981 and was shipped to Hong Kong in 1983. Design 980 on Chassis 5AT 72 has vanished, but curiously the landaulette was returned to Hooper & Co in 1993 for total restoration, with a mileage of only 16,000. (In the boot was found a rather desiccated lizard!) Whilst shipping the 1965 landaulette back to the United Kingdom in 1993, the stevedores knocked the front windscreen out and ran a rope through, past the division, in order to hook the limousine on board.

SOUTH AFRICA

The government of South Africa has had a long history of careful maintenance of its Rolls-Royce fleet, although the last limousine was pensioned off in 1963. Since then, a succession of Mercedes-Benz and other vehicles has been supplied, and at present the President uses a BMW. Rolls-Royce took over from Daimler in the mid- twenties, with the latter company making a brief reappearance some twenty years later.

The first delivery was probably an early Silver Ghost, a 1909 Barker

The Governor-General of the Union of South Africa travels by 40/50hp Silver Ghost tourer to the Empire Exhibition celebrating Johannesburg's 50th anniversary, in 1936. Note the crown, flagstaff and front-wheel brakes.

This unidentified Phantom I carries a very old-fashioned landaulette body
with vee windscreen, coach handles on the doors and wide running boards.
The landaulette portion provides a good view of the occupants.

limousine on chassis 1190, which was used by Lord Gladstone to open the first 'Union' Parliament in 1910. Gladstone also had use of an 'Alpine Eagle' type Silver Ghost. Some time later the Governor-General acquired an updated Silver Ghost which had quite a long life, and was in the style of a landaulette. Full four-wheel braking had been introduced in 1924, to general acclaim, and quite a few models were recalled to Derby for retrospective attention. However, 79 EU was not amongst these, it came from the last sanction of the series which had four wheel brakes. Certainly to dispose of a Silver Ghost used generally for state occasions after just fifteen years would seem, on the face of it, to be a bit over-cautious. Chassis number 79 EU is known for this late car, but the one recorded for the landaulette was 119 RC. However, this vehicle would seem to be the incorrect one as that car is in fact a Freestone & Webb saloon. The Earl of Clarendon probably used both cars though, and the file runs from 1931 to 1937. The landaulette, meanwhile, was still in use up to the outbreak of World War II.

One is certainly on firmer ground as regards the delivery of the first Rolls-Royce V-12, chassis 3BT 25, which was handed over to the Governor-General's office in April 1937. It had originally been tested at Hooper & Co on the 5 February. The Phantom III was a landaulette and fitted with crowns on front and rear bumpers, blue police light to roof and one side-mounted spare to the near side. The car was later modified to

The 1937 Phantom III, chassis 3BT 25, originally used by the Governor-General of South Africa still survives in Germany. It is now painted in less sombre colours and no longer has the police lamp and trumpet horns.

The Governor-General of South Africa travelling in his 1937 Phantom III, chassis 3BT 25. The Hooper landaulette coachwork was to design 69Z7 and was body no. 8801. Note the crown, police lamp and absence of a mascot.

solid tappets and had 3ins higher headroom. The Phantom was finished in dark blue and black and mainly used by Sir Patrick Duncan, the first South African to hold the post of Governor-General. The vehicle was sold in the Windhoek area in the late fifties, and is now owned by a German collector.

The South African Government placed an order for a Park Ward lan-daulette in the autumn of 1956. This was chassis FLW 63 and had the unusual addition of an oval-shaped blue priority light above the windscreen so that the car could be given special treatment on the move. The Governor-General at that time was E.J. Jansen who was followed by the

The Governor-General of South Africa's Silver Wraith long wheelbase Park Ward landaulette on chassis FLW 63. When the rear compartment hood was closed it offered full weather protection. Note the huge blue identification lamp above the windscreen.

The ex-South African Silver Wraith, chassis FLW 63, survives in a German collection and has been repainted. Post-war Park Ward bodies were not noted for their styling, particularly from the rear.

man who took South Africa out of the Commonwealth, C.R. Swart. In 1963, South Africa sold the Park Ward landaulette to a Mrs Potter who then sold it in 1988 to another German collector. Sadly, the car has not moved in the following years.

SUDAN

The Governor of the Sudan ordered a Rolls-Royce in the autumn of 1954. The Anglo-Egyptian Condominium which had controlled the huge territory from the beginning of the century had been dissolved and the Sudan became officially independent in 1952, a Republic a few years later. The population is now about 27 million, in nearly a million square miles, the largest country in Africa.

In late 1944, the then Governor of the Sudan purchased an H.J. Mulliner Phantom III on chassis 3BU 40 to bodywork number 4466 from the estate of Mrs. Hamilton-Gore. This was a seven-seater limousine, or rather a four-light saloon with division, which had been delivered on 22 February 1937 to Mrs L.H. Gault. This vehicle was replaced some ten years later by a Silver Wraith.

In January 1955, the Governor had just taken delivery of a Park Ward-bodied limousine to design 551 on chassis DLW 61. This vehicle was a popular design and the British Ambassador in Egypt had such a vehicle. The car may well have been taken over by the British Ambassador in Khartoum. Whatever the outcome, I can recall that a great many limousines, some of Rolls-Royce manufacture, were sent to be sold in the United Kingdom at this time and this limousine may well have been one of them. Regrettably, the fate of the Park Ward vehicle is unknown.

Finally, the Republic of the Sudan took delivery of an H.J. Mulliner drophead coupé, on the Silver Cloud II chassis SWC 122, in October 1960. The curious fact about this vehicle is that some years ago an eminent professor was offered the car in part-payment for some telecommunications work. Sadly he did not arrange to fly the vehicle to safer territory where it it might well have survived the ensuing civil war and continuing unrest.

TANZANIA

Formerly known as Tanganyika, Tanzania was founded in December 1962 and became a Republic some twelve months later. Three years afterwards, the Sultanate of Zanzibar was absorbed to form the United Republic of Tanzania.

The only known Phantom to be acquired by the President of Tanzania was the first State Landaulette to the H.J. Mulliner Park Ward design 2052,

RIGHT TOP, AND FOLLOWING PAGES: *The President of Tanzania took delivery of the very first Phantom V ceremonial State Landaulette (chassis 5VD 99, body S34) in 1965. The hood folded back from the division and had a PVC rear window. Unlike all later bodies to design 2052 there was no glass roof panel over the front compartment.*
RIGHT BOTTOM: *With the hood mechanism, extra electrics and air conditioning unit, luggage space was minimal. Pouches were provided for shields and flagmasts.*

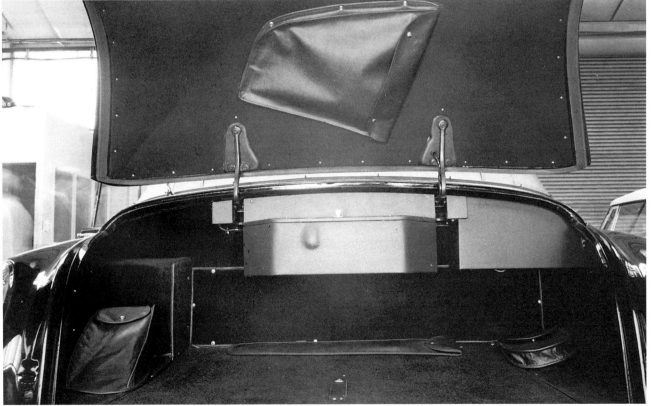

*On Phantom V State Landaulette 5VD 99 a Jet Star air conditioning unit
replaced the picnic table under the facia. White switches above the umbrella
handbrake raise the rear seat and operate the hood over rear compartment.*

In front compartment roof of State Landaulette 5VD 99 are the recessed micro-phone so that the chauffeur can communicate with the rear passengers and the knurled knob for securing the roof-mounted illuminated shield.

The rear compartment of the President of Tanzania's Phantom V ceremonial State Landaulette, chassis 5VD 99. With a width of only 45.5 inches between the side armrests (above), the rear seat was designed for two people. The handset for the Redifon radio telephone is in the front of the armrest (left of picture) with the heater/air conditioning controls above. Grilles below seat are for the recirculatory heater. The microphone for the intercom (right) is in the front of the nearside armrest with the radio set in a veneered panel above.

and this was on chassis 5VD 99. The second State landaulette (5DV 83), on the stand at the 1965 Earls Court Motor Show, was eventually purchased by the East Nigerian government and delivered in March 1966.

The original requirement had been for a cabriolet but the hood was too large. This was solved by designing the hood to fold back from behind the division and not cover the whole of the seating space. A transparent panel was added over the driver's head.

Chassis 5VD 99 progressed through the Willesden works. Both cars had been started in 1965 but the President of Tanzania received his first in September that year. The export price without VAT at this time was quoted at £16,225, whereas a standard Phantom retailed at only £7,875 tax-free. The Tanzanian car was air-conditioned in both front and back, and the rear seat could be raised or lowered at will. Affixed in the central portion of the roof was a Tanzanian heraldic shield with a facility to fly the standard just to the rear. The driver received his instructions from the rear seat, whilst the Presidential Palace kept in touch via the radio-telephone whose aerial was easily removable from the saddle panel at the rear of the car. Two wing-mounted flag masts were also included in the specification.

The Phantom V State landaulette is still alive and well and recent attention will probably ensure that it stays that way. The main problems seem to centre around the power-steering and air-conditioning systems, but the car has already completed well over 40,000 miles.

TUNISIA

Tunisia lies between Algeria and Libya. One of the first tasks of its government, established in 1956, was to abolish the monarchy. This was easily achieved by such a formidable politician as President Bourguiba, who eventually was declared President for life in 1975. In late 1987, however, Bourguiba was deposed (by his Prime Minister General Ben Ali) and the present administration took over.

Very soon after coming to power the 1956 Tunisian Government

FOLLOWING PAGES: *Phantom V Park Ward landaulette, to design 1000, on chassis 5LCG 51 for the President of Tunisia.*

209

ordered a Phantom V landaulette to the design 1000 on chassis 5LCG 51. The car, not unlike that used by HM The Queen Mother, was fitted with a hammered landaulette leather head and equipped with a flagmast to both front wings. The car's interior was fitted with a communication system for talking to the driver, a drinks cabinet in the rear and, with the terrific heat of North Africa in mind, air-conditioning. A set of loose covers and a rear compartment radio set were also provided. The car was handed over to the Government in Tunis in May 1962.

The car probably does survive as it was last seen in a long procession of vehicles leaving the dockside during The Queen's visit in 1980. But nobody in authority can confirm whether the vehicle is still in the country fifteen years later.

UGANDA

After some seventy years of British Rule, Uganda became a republic in October 1962. On the face of it, the Government's decision to purchase a Rolls-Royce in late 1964 was a little unexpected and may well have been prompted by the acquisition of Rolls-Royces by neighbouring countries.

The H.J. Mulliner Park Ward seven-passenger limousine, design 2003, had a very high profile in the country and the Phantom V, on chassis number 5VD 27, was delivered in January 1965. As with so many limousines of this design, no further trace of the car can now be found. (The bloody regime of Idi Amin began with the coup of 1971.)

ZAMBIA

The Republic of Zambia, formerly Northern Rhodesia, came into being on 24 October 1964. Its capital is Lusaka, and the population was seven-and-a-half million in the late eighties.

The Park Ward style of landaulette, to design 727, was a very popular creation and especially so when one considered the size of hats worn by the Governor's consorts. Chassis FLW 86 was fitted with front and rear illuminated crowns, plus a roof fitment for holding a standard. The completed car was handed over to the then Governor of the colony in May 1957 and, rather surprisingly, the vehicle was not disposed of until after the arrival of a Phantom V in 1967. The Silver Wraith landaulette was then shipped out of Zambia via Rhodesia (as was) and later took part in the 1973 Alpine Rally. It was sold in Britain at the end of the decade. The final Rolls-Royce Phantom V was on chassis 5VF 133 which, with its H.J. Mulliner Park Ward body to design 2003, was handed over to the President in July 1967. Unfortunately, it is not known if the Phantom V limousine survives.

ZIMBABWE

Zimbabwe, formerly known as Rhodesia, came into being in 1980, following elections in February that year. Earlier, before the Unilateral Declaration of Independence in 1965, Park Ward were called in to supply a landaulette for the use of the Governor-General of Rhodesia. This was chassis FLW 78, a Silver Wraith often used for visits by other heads of state and prime ministers. (The car was employed during the ill-fated talks which took place in Salisbury during a visit by Harold Wilson). The landaulette was fitted with twin forward roof lights, behind which could be flown a flag. For some strange reason, the front bumpers had an attachment for reflecting lights. I am happy to report that the 1957 Silver Wraith was retained for Presidential use, with Robert Mugabe occupying that post after 25 years of a declared state of emergency and election victory in 1990. There must be very few state cars which have survived a Unilateral Declaration of Independence, international sanctions, several elections, continuous struggle between two political parties that finally merged, to still be at the disposal of the President. A suitable vehicle, perhaps, with which to end an A to Z of Rolls-Royce state motor cars, one that has witnessed the gamut of political changes, impervious to each. Viewers of the Harare Commonwealth Conference in 1991 would have seen Her Majesty The Queen using the Silver Wraith Park Ward landaulette during her visit.

Silver Wraith Park Ward landaulette, to design 727 on chassis FLW 86, originally supplied to the Governor of Northern Rhodesia (now Zambia) in 1957. It later returned to Britain and was pictured at the Rolls-Royce Enthusiasts' Club's annual rally at Blenheim Palace in June 1971. The usual chrome waistrail moulding has been extended to include the bonnet on this car.

The HERALD   Mon 25/6/84

President to open Parliament

CDE Canaan Banana will tomorrow open the fifth session of the first Parliament of Zimbabwe.

In a one-hour rehearsal yesterday (above), mounted police accompanied the President's car past Parliament Buildings while the army band played the national anthem.

MARCHED

At the start of the rehearsal, the guard of honour and the Signals Band marched to the Parliament Buildings in Baker Avenue.

● The public is advised that certain roads will be closed to traffic from 6 am to 2 pm for the opening of Parliament tomorrow, the police have announced.

The closures are: Third Street at Union Avenue; Gordon Avenue at Third Street; Stanley Avenue at Third Street; and Baker Avenue at Second and Third streets. — Herald Reporter-Ziana.

The Silver Wraith Park Ward landaulette, chassis FLW 78, supplied to the Governor-General of Rhodesia in 1957 still survives, used by President Mugabe. It is pictured in use for Canaan Banana's rehearsal for the opening of Parliament in June 1984.

CHASSIS RECORDS

Year	Chassis	Country	Coachbuilder and body type
Silver Ghost			
1919	?	Romania	Barker limousine
1919	?	Romania	Barker torpedo tourer
1914	40 RB	Russia	Kellner limousine
1922	33 KG	Australia	HJ Mulliner tourer
1926	S338 RK	Cuba	Merrimac Oxford tourer
1909	1113	India	Barker landaulette
1923	38 PG	Iran	Hooper landaulette
1921	21 UE	Japan	Hooper limousine
1921	38 UE	Japan	Hooper limousine
1923	58 YG	Japan	Hooper tourer
1921	108 AG	Thailand	Hooper cabriolet
1920	54 FW	Kenya	Labourdette
1914	12 YB	Egypt	Rothschild limousine
1915	31 ED	Egypt	Brewster/Hooper limousine
1925	79 EU	South Africa	Unknown tourer
20HP			
1923	48 GO	Greece	Cockshoot landaulette
1923	66 H1	Sweden	Unknown limousine
1923	52 S8	Afghanistan	Barker tourer
1928	GBM 44	Afghanistan	Barker 2-door saloon
1926	GUK 51	Singapore	Barker landaulette
Phantom I			
1926	60 YC	Afghanistan	Barker sports
1927	112 NC	Afghanistan	Hooper tourer
1928	38 UF	Afghanistan	Barker landaulette

Year	Chassis	Country	Coachbuilder and body type
1928	3 AL	Afghanistan	Barker cabriolet
1926	72 DC	Iran	Hooper limousine
1928	88 UF	Iraq	Fountains tourer
1926	66 TC	Hejaz/S. Arabia	Thrupp & Maberly
1926	66 TC	Hejaz/S. Arabia	Thrupp & Maberly
1926	118 HC	Egypt	Hooper limousine
1929	22 OR	Egypt	Hooper landaulette
1925	101 MC	Ceylon/Sri Lanka	Barker landaulette

Phantom II

Year	Chassis	Country	Coachbuilder and body type
1932	223 AMS	Poland	Barker tourer
1930	178 GY	Siam/Thailand	Saoutchik limousine
1930	30 GY	Egypt	Hooper limousine
1930	6 XJ	Ethiopia	Hooper landaulette (dickey)
1935	33 TA	Dominican Rep	Hooper limousine

20/25 HP

Year	Chassis	Country	Coachbuilder and body type
1935	GLG 38	Thailand	Hooper limousine
1930	GLR 62	Egypt	Hooper limousine

Phantom III

Year	Chassis	Country	Coachbuilder and body type
1937	3BT 131	Belgium	Vesters & Neirick limousine
1938	3DL 102	Greece	HJ Mulliner/Hooper
1939	3DL 142	Greece	HJ Mulliner saloon
1938	3CM 81	Poland	Vanooren 2-seater dhc
1938	3 CP 116	Portugal	Windovers/Hooper cabriolet
1936	3AZ 50	Romania	Gurney Nutting 2-seater dhc
1937	3CP 34	Romania	Park Ward touring limousine
1938	3 DL 2	Australia	Hooper limousine
1939	3DL 200	Afghanistan	Park Ward drophead coupé
1936	3AZ 47	India	Hooper limousine
1939	3DL 138	Iran	Park Ward touring limousine
1937	3 BU 132	Iraq	Hooper limousine
1937	3 AZ 202	Iraq	G. Nutting sedanca de ville

Year	Chassis	Country	Coachbuilder and body type
1938	3 CM 197	Iraq	Hooper sedanca de ville
1938	3 CM 145	Iraq	Hooper limousine
1937	3 BT 193	Malaysia	Hooper limousine
1937	3CM 25	Saudi Arabia	Hooper cabriolet
1937	3BT 97	Singapore	Hooper limousine
1939	3 DL 158	Thailand	HJ Mulliner limousine de ville
1938	3CM 63	Egypt	Hooper limousine
1940	3DL 182	Egypt	Charlesworth limousine
1937	3BT 25	South Africa	Hooper landaulette
1937	3BU 40	Sudan	HJ Mulliner limousine

Wraith

Year	Chassis	Country	Coachbuilder and body type
1939	WEC 17	Iraq	Hooper sedanca de ville
1939	WEC 5	Iraq	Hooper limousine

Silver Wraith

Year	Chassis	Country	Coachbuilder and body type
1947	WVA 12	Belgium	HJ Mulliner saloon
1947	WVA 41	Belgium	Park Ward limousine
1948	WYA 5	Belgium	Van den Plas cabriolet
1958	LGLW 25	Denmark	Hooper limousine
1959	LHLW 44	Greece	Hooper allweather (Perspex)
1949	WGC 1	Ireland	Hooper landaulette
1958	LGLW 24	Netherlands	Park Ward landaulette
1948	WCB 17	Spain	HJ Mulliner sedanca de ville
1953	LBLW 37	Yugoslavia	HJ Mulliner cabriolet
1954	DLW 24	Australia	Park Ward limousine
1959	HLW 47	Australia	Hooper cabriolet
1959	HLW 49	Australia	Hooper cabriolet
1958	HLW 45	Australia	HJ Mulliner limousine
1958	HLW 46	Australia	HJ Mulliner limousine
1958	HLW 48	Australia	HJ Mulliner limousine
1958	HLW 50	Australia	HJ Mulliner limousine
1948	WCB 32	Argentina	HJ Mulliner sedanca de ville
1953	LWSG 53	Brazil	HJ Mulliner touring limousine

Year	Chassis	Country	Coachbuilder and body type
1953	LWSG 74	Brazil	HJ Mulliner touring limousine
1952	LALW 27	Brazil	HJ Mulliner limousine
1953	LALW 29	Brazil	HJ Mulliner cabriolet
1954	LDLW 60	Venezuela	Hooper touring limousine
1955	LELW 16	Venezuela	Hooper limousine
1951	WME 66	Buganda(Burundi)	HJ Mulliner touring limousine
1952	ALW 28	Bahrain	HJ Mulliner limousine
1952	WOF 46	Qatar	Park Ward limousine
1954	LBLW 57	Qatar	Hooper touring limousine
1947	WVA 6	India	Park Ward limousine
1955	DLW 99	Hong Kong	HJ Mulliner touring limousine
1952	LALW 31	Iraq	Franay sedanca de ville
1947	WTA 50	Iraq	Hooper touring limousine
1957	FLW 90	Japan	Hooper limousine
1958	GLW 22	Malaysia	HJ Mulliner limousine
1950	WHD 52	Malaysia	Park Ward limousine
1948	WZB 7	Pakistan	Hooper touring limousine
1954	BLW 92	Singapore	Hooper landaulette
1948	WYA 1	Ceylon/Sri Lanka	HJ Mulliner sedanca de ville
1947	WVA 40	Ceylon/Sri Lanka	Hooper touring limousine
1959	LHLW 51	Ethiopia	Hooper allweather
1954	CLW 36	Ethiopia	Park Ward landaulette
1955	DLW 82	Ethiopia	HJ Mulliner sports limousine
1953	ALW 32	G. Coast/Ghana	HJ M. pullman landaulette
1955	DLW 126	G. Coast/Ghana	Park Ward landaulette
1957	FLW 61	G. Coast/Ghana	Park Ward landaulette
1957	FLW 72	G. Coast/Ghana	HJ Mulliner touring limousine
1957	FLW 75	Nyasaland/Malawi	Park Ward landaulette
1957	LFLW 80	Morocco	James Young limousine
1952	ALW 11	Nigeria	Hooper cabriolet
1955	ELW 4	W. Nigeria	Park Ward limousine
1958	ELW 55	Nigeria	Hooper landaulette
1958	HLW 35	W.Nigeria	Hooper landaulette
1957	FLW 63	South Africa	Park Ward landaulette

Year	Chassis	Country	Coachbuilder and body type
1955	DLW 61	Sudan	Park Ward limousine
1957	FLW 86	N.Rhodesia/Zambia	Park Ward landaulette
1957	FLW 78	Rhodesia/Zimbabwe	Park Ward landaulette

Silver Dawn

Year	Chassis	Country	Coachbuilder and body type
1954	LSOG 54	Nicaragua	Park Ward
1952	SFC 118	Gibraltar	Rolls-Royce saloon
1954	SUJ 24	Malta	Rolls-Royce saloon

Phantom IV

Year	Chassis	Country	Coachbuilder and body type
1952	4AF 14	Spain	HJ Mulliner limousine
1952	4AF 16	Spain	HJ Mulliner limousine
1952	4AF 18	Spain	HJ Mulliner cabriolet
1951	4AF 6	Iran	HJ Mulliner 2-door cabriolet
1956	4CS 6	Iran	Hooper limousine
1953	4BP 1	Iraq	Hooper touring limousine
1953	4BP 3	Iraq	Hooper touring limousine
1951	4AF 8	Kuwait	HJ Mulliner saloon
1955	4CS 2	Kuwait	HJ Mulliner limousine
1956	4CS 4	Kuwait	HJ Mulliner limousine
1952	4AF 22	Saudi Arabia	Franay allweather

Silver Cloud

Year	Chassis	Country	Coachbuilder and body type
1958	LSGE 252	Iraq	Hooper drophead coupé
1956	SWA 100	Iraq	Hooper touring limousine
1958	SGE 310	Ghana	HJ Mulliner drophead coupé

Silver Cloud II

Year	Chassis	Country	Coachbuilder and body type
1960	LSWC 418	Iran	HJ Mulliner dhc
1960	SWC 122	Sudan	HJ Mulliner dhc

Silver Cloud III

Year	Chassis	Country	Coachbuilder and body type
1965	LSHS 329C	Greece	Mulliner Park Ward dhc
1963	CAL 37	Australia	MPW 4-door cabriolet

Year	Chassis	Country	Coachbuilder and body type
1963	CAL 39	Australia	MPW 4-door cabriolet
1964	SGT 593C	Bahrain	MPW dhc

Silver Cloud III lwb

Year	Chassis	Country	Coachbuilder and body type
1964	CDL 3	Malawi	MPW 4-door cabriolet
1964	LCDL 1	Morocco	James Young touring limousine

Phantom V

Year	Chassis	Country	Coachbuilder and body type
1960	5 LAT 84	Portugal	Park Ward limousine
1967	5 LVF 113	Romania	MPW State landaulette
1960	5 LAT 6	Yugoslavia	Park Ward limousine
1967	5 VF 155	Australia	MPW limousine
1967	5 VF 159	Australia	MPW limousine
1962	5 VA 5	New Zealand	MPW limousine
1962	5 VA 15	New Zealand	MPW limousine
1961	5LBX 30	Dominican Rep	Park Ward limousine
1965	5 LVD 33	Bahrain	MPW landaulette
1966	5 VD 83	Bahrain	MPW State landaulette
1966	5 LVF 67	Bahrain	MPW limousine
1961	5 BV 7	Hong Kong	Park Ward landaulette
1962	5 LCG 51	Tunisia	Park Ward landaulette
1960	5 LAS 39	Iran	Park Ward limousine
1966	5 LVF 29	Iran	MPW State landaulette
1961	5 LBV 91	Japan	Park Ward 8-pass limousine
1961	5 LVA 29	Japan	MPW limousine
1960	5 LBV 5	Jordan	MPW limousine
1967	5 LVF 139	Jordan	MPW limousine
1967	5 LVF 123	Kuwait	MPW limousine
1964	5 VC 47	Sabah (Malaysia)	MPW limousine
1963	5VA 45	Malaysia	MPW limousine
1964	5VC 45	Malaysia	MPW limousine
1968	5VF 169	Malaysia	MPW limousine
1967	5 VF 163	Pakistan	MPW limousine
1962	5LCG 3	Saudi Arabia	Park Ward limousine

Year	Chassis	Country	Coachbuilder
1966	5VF 31	Singapore	MPW limousine
1963	5VA 95	Kenya	MPW limousine
1963	5LVA 37	Liberia	MPW limousine
1962	5LCG 53	Libya	Park Ward limousine
1968	5VF 181	Malawi	MPW limousine
1963	5LVA 41	Morocco	James Young touring lim.
1960	5AS 75	N.Nigeria	Park Ward limousine
1960	5AT 72	N.Nigeria	Park Ward limousine
1960	5AT 96	Nigeria	Park Ward limousine
1961	5BX 46	N.Nigeria	Park Ward limousine
1965	5DV 41	Nigeria	MPW landaulette
1965	5VD 27	Uganda	MPW limousine
1965	5VD 99	Tanzania	MPW State Landaulette
1966	5VE 15	Abu Dhabi (UAE)	MPW limousine
1967	5VF 133	Zambia	MPW limousine

Phantom VI

Year	Chassis	Country	Coachbuilder
1973	PRH 4857	Australia	MPW limousine
1975	PRH 4822	W. Australia	MPW limousine
1976	PRH 4839	Australia (NSW)	MPW limousine
1970	PRH 4582	New Zealand	MPW limousine
1970	PRH 4583	New Zealand	MPW limousine
1972	PRX 4720	Bahrain	MPW limousine
1971	PRH 4642	Brunei	MPW limousine
1974	PRH 4793	Brunei	MPW State Landaulette
1991	LWH 10426	Brunei	MPW Landaulette
1977	PRX 4860	Iran	Mulliner Park Ward
1977	PRX 4861	Iran	Mulliner Park Ward
1977	PRX 4857	Kuwait	MPW limousine
1971	PRH 4668	Malaysia	MPW limousine
1986	GWH 10153	Malaysia	MPW State Landaulette
1971	PRX 4633	Saudi Arabia	MPW limousine
1972	PRH 4713	Saudi Arabia	MPW limousine
1975	PRX 4802	Saudi Arabia	MPW limousine

Year	Chassis	Country	Coachbuilder
1975	PRX 4803	Saudi Arabia	MPW limousine
1974	PRX 4808	Saudi Arabia	MPW limousine
1974	PRX 4809	Saudi Arabia	MPW limousine
1975	PRX 4819	Saudi Arabia	MPW limousine
1975	PRH 4828	Saudi Arabia	MPW limousine
1977	PRX 4853	Saudi Arabia	MPW limousine
1978	PRX 4853	Saudi Arabia	MPW limousine
1978	PRX 4856	Saudi Arabia	MPW limousine
1978	PRX 4869	Saudi Arabia	MPW limousine
1973	PRH 4732	Japan	MPW limousine
1973	PRH 4765	Thailand	MPW limousine
1973	PRH 4769	Thailand	MPW limousine
1980	PGH 115	Thailand	MPW limousine
1972	PRX 4664	Gabon	MPW limousine
1972	PRH 4716	Gabon	MPW State Landaulette
1976	PRX 4844	Gabon	MPW limousine
1977	PRX 4845	Gabon	MPW limousine
1976	PRX 4849	Qatar	MPW limousine

Silver Shadow

Year	Chassis	Country	Coachbuilder
?	?	Bahrain	MPW Park Ward lwb saloon
1975	LRX 22245	Cent Afr Rep	Mulliner Park Ward
1977	SRH 300	Thailand	Rolls-Royce Motors saloon

Corniche III

Year	Chassis	Country	Coachbuilder
1980	MCH 30350	Japan	MPW convertible
1990	LCH 30285	Thailand	MPW convertible

Silver Spur III

Year	Chassis	Country	Coachbuilder
1991	MCH 32592	Thailand	Rolls-Royce Motor Cars saloon
1991	MCH 32595	Thailand	Rolls-Royce Motor Cars saloon
1994	?	Denmark	Rolls-Royce Motor Cars saloon

One of the King of Thailand's Phantom VIs with H.J. Mulliner, Park Ward limousine body. Note the fitments for mounting flags just behind the headlamps and the mirrors on the wing crowns. This is probably chassis PRH 4767 delivered in 1973. (See page 161.)